CYPRUS

THE ISLANDS SERIES

*Published in the United States by Stackpole
†Published in the United States by David & Charles
‡Distributed in Australia by Wren Publishing Pty Ltd
  Melbourne

CYPRUS

by MICHAEL and HANKA LEE

DAVID & CHARLES

NEWTON ABBOT

ISBN 0 7153 5980 0

Set in eleven on thirteen point Baskerville
and printed in Great Britain
by Latimer Trend & Company Ltd Plymouth
for David & Charles (Holdings) Limited
South Devon House   Newton Abbot   Devon

CONTENTS

ILLUSTRATIONS

7

ILLUSTRATIONS

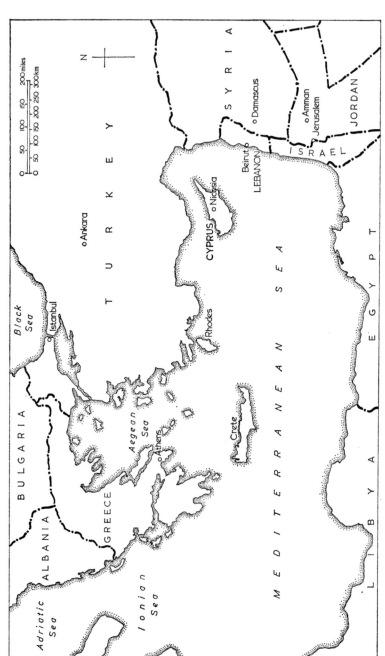

THE EASTERN MEDITERRANEAN

1   THE ISLAND OF APHRODITE

CYPRUS is an island of contrasts, presenting different faces to different people. It is a land where East meets West: although culturally and politically a part of Europe, geologically it is in Asia. Situated in the extreme eastern corner of the Mediterranean, Cyprus is only 40 miles south of the Anatolian coast of Turkey at its closest point, 60 miles west of Syria and 150 miles north of the Nile Delta.

To all who touch upon its shores, Cyprus is, first and foremost, a place of gentle charm. Leonardo da Vinci remarked in his *Notebooks* that 'here the beauty of some pleasant hill invites the wandering mariners to take their ease among its flowery verdure, where the zephyrs continually come and go, filling with sweet odours the island and the encompassing sea'. Other distinguished visitors to Cyprus, from Homer and Euripides to Disraeli and Durrell, have written with enthusiasm about its beauty. Indeed, it was here that Aphrodite, Goddess of Love, was born, at Petra tou Romiou, under the white cliffs of Paphos. This, too, was the island of which Mark Antony made a gift to Cleopatra and her sister, Arsinoe. It was in the mountains in the north of the island that Walt Disney found the setting that inspired his film *Snow White and the Seven Dwarfs*. Rimbaud sought peace from the troubles of contemporary life in the central Troodos range. And now Cyprus is becoming a holiday island for tens of thousands of tourists, who return to its shores year after year.

To the strategists and statesmen of both East and West, the island has long been regarded as a possession of great value.

For, not only does it contain important raw materials—copper, asbestos and timber—but, due to its location, it has offered the opportunity for economic and political control of the Levant. According to Gustav Hirschfeld, writing at the end of the nineteenth century, 'he who would become and remain a great power in the east must hold Cyprus in his hand. That this is true, is proved by the history of the world during the last three and one half millennia'. Indeed, throughout the eighty centuries of its recorded history, the island was never self-determining, finally achieving independence as the Republic of Cyprus in 1960. From the fourteen century BC it was colonised successively by Myceneans, Ionians, Phoenicians and Persians. It was captured by the Egyptian Ptolemies, later annexed by Rome, attacked by the Saracens, then came under the English crown for a period of less than a year. Between 1192 and 1489 Cyprus was ruled by the Lusignan dynasty, after which it was captured by the Republic of Venice. It was incorporated into the Ottoman Empire in 1572 until, in the final phase of its history of colonial occupation, it became part of the British Empire from 1878 up to independence.

Although the native culture of the Cypriots has remained remarkably unscathed by the succession of foreign rulers, each of these great civilisations has left some physical reminders of its influence on the island. Certainly, earthquakes have damaged a number of the antiquities; and past lack of concern for the historical value of many buildings has meant that either they have been allowed to decay or have been demolished in the cause of 'progress'. Looters, too, have carried off much of the more spectacular treasure for, until the Antiquities Law was passed in 1904, two-thirds of all treasure discovered could legally be removed from the island. But Cyprus remains one vast archaeological site: it is said now to accommodate a higher density of foreign archaeologists than any other comparable area in the world.

Many Bronze Age tombs still hide their contents of pottery

and golden jewellery; Greek amphoras lie on the sea-bed in their thousands. Roman amphitheatres have been restored for contemporary use, and Byzantine churches and monasteries in all parts of the island still resound to the music of medieval chants. Even the fortifications built by the Lusignans and Venetians in the fourteenth and fifteenth centuries were brought back into use in the middle of the twentieth century for the defence of particularly important strategic positions.

To Greece and Turkey Cyprus remains a potential source of conflict. Events in Cyprus in the 1950s and 1960s were close to bringing the two countries to war. The reasons for this confrontation lie deep in the island's history: since the arrival of the first Greek colonists in the fourteenth century BC, the majority of Cypriots have been educated into Greek cultural traditions, speaking the Greek language and keeping to their own religion. (But although the Greek-speaking Cypriots do claim a descent from these original colonists, this is belied by many family names—Daveronas, Romanos, Attalides and the like, clearly deriving from times of various subsequent foreign occupations.) The Turkish-speaking minority, on the other hand, did not settle in Cyprus until the time of the Ottoman occupation, and have never become fully assimilated with the Greeks. Apart from the traditional enmity of Greeks and Turks which largely springs from religious differences, the underlying cause of tension in the island was the long-standing dream of the Greek Cypriots for union of Cyprus with Greece. The demands reached a climax between 1955 and 1959, with the anti-British guerilla activities of the underground organisation EOKA. The Turkish Cypriots took no part in the hostilities, but moved from an initial position of neutrality towards the Greek Cypriots to one of hostility. For, if Cyprus were to be united with Greece, this, they claim, would lead to a partial loss of their rights. The differences between the two communities eventually resulted in intermittent, although severe, intercommunal fighting in the 1960s.

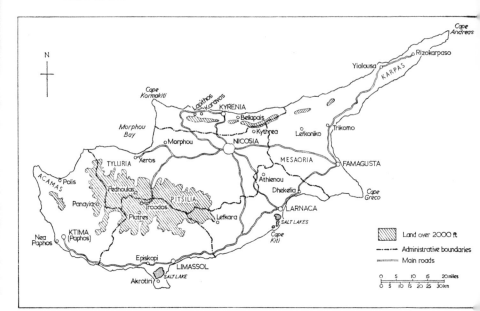

TOPOGRAPHY AND PLACE-NAMES

A VIEW OF THE ISLAND

Cyprus has thus won for itself an importance out of all proportion to its size. It is the third largest island in the Mediterranean, smaller only than Sicily and Sardinia, with a total land area of 3,572 square miles. In size it is equivalent to the combined areas of the counties of Kent, Surrey and Sussex, or rather less than half the size of the state of Massachusetts. The shape of Cyprus was compared by the ancients to an outstretched deer-skin—with the peninsula of the Karpas in the north east as the tail. The maximum length of the island is about 140 miles, between Cape Andreas at the end of the Karpas and Petra tou Romiou in the south west. From north to south the width is never more than 60 miles.

A little under half of the island is under cultivation as arable land, devoted in part to the citrus fruits and vines for which

14

Cyprus is justly famed and, more extensively, to cereals, which are the main cash crop. One-fifth of the island is afforested, a much smaller portion than in earlier centuries but, despite a high incidence of fires, afforestation is gradually being extended. The remaining one-third is either developed for human settlements, is marginal land used for occasional grazing of sheep or goats, or else, like large parts of the coastal area, is completely unproductive. There are no perennial rivers on the island, although it can boast of two large salt lakes. One of these, near Larnaca, is used for the commercial extraction of salt; the other, near Limassol, is unexploited.

Such a bare statement of the vital statistics of the island necessarily conceals the fact that there are considerable regional variations in topography and soils, hence in vegetation, economic life and cultural characteristics. These differences are caused mainly by the presence of two mountain formations. The larger and more extensive of the two is the Troodos massif, lying in the western half of the island and rising to a maximum height of 6,403ft on Mount Olympus. The Kyrenia range, on the other hand, is much lower, rising only to 3,360ft. The latter forms a needle-sharp ridge running for almost a hundred miles along the northern coast, separated from the sea by only a narrow belt of fertile land. East and south of these two groups lies the plain of the Mesaoria, meaning literally 'Between the Mountains'; this is the agricultural heart of Cyprus.

The Troodos massif itself occupies around one-third of the island's surface, approximately 1,250 square miles. A little below the pine-clad summit of Mount Olympus is the once-fashionable summer resort of the village of Troodos. But apart from this and a small handful of other settlements on the south and east, the area is sparsely inhabited in its upper reaches, since the rocky terrain does not allow for easy cultivation. The lower slopes, however, are thick with orchards of peach and plum, apricot and almond, with narrow straggling terraces of vines, concealing picturesque little villages, ruined monasteries

15

covered with Byzantine frescoes, and even mines that may hark back to Roman or Phoenician days. At places throughout these mountains, too, can be found working mines of copper or chrome; and, at Amiandos, an open-cast asbestos mine.

The Kyrenia range, although much less extensive, has its own peculiar Gothic attractions. It offers, on one side, a view of the Mesaoria plain: seen in the summer from the moist coolness of the mountains as a shimmering haze of dust, and virtually featureless except for the small villages of mud which blend imperceptibly into the landscape; and in the winter and spring, as a green mass of cornfields. On the other side of the mountains can be seen glimpses of the jaggedly carved coastline of the island, with views across the sea to the snow-capped mountains of Anatolia, 40 miles distant.

This range, like the Troodos region, has been made accessible to motorists and walkers by the construction of a network of forestry roads. These gravelled tracks lead along the ridge, linking the three medieval castles of St Hilarion, Buffavento and Kantara, and pass through the forests of pine and cypress, past the white peaks of Pentadactylos ('Five Fingers') and Qartal Dagh, both circled by eagles and vultures. Side roads lead off to the fourteenth-century Armenian monastery of Sourp Magar and, farther east, to the painted church of Antiphonitis.

On the slopes of the mountains facing the sea lie a number of the most attractive villages in the island: Lapithos, surrounded by lemon groves; Karmi, on which the sun never rises in the winter months; Trapeza, abandoned by its population after the intercommunal fighting of the 1960s; and Bellapais, probably the island's best-known village, for it was here that Lawrence Durrell made his home, which he describes so vividly in *Bitter Lemons*. The focal point of Bellapais is the ruined abbey, said to be the finest example of Gothic architecture in the Middle East, and from it—the Abbaye de la Paix—the village derives its name. The abbey stands on the edge of a cliff over-

Page 17 Kyrenia from the air. This small harbour town, on the north coast and only 16 miles from Nicosia, is a popular seaside resort

Page 18 (above) The remains of Neolithic houses at Khirokitia; (below) Remains of the Temple of Apollo, near Curium, where Apollo Hylates was worshipped as the city god

looking the sea; the architecture, the dark cypress trees planted in its courtyard and the magnificent view together create a remarkable ensemble. The village itself, typical of those in the Kyrenia mountains, lies on a steep slope, with stone-built houses fronting on to narrow streets, and everywhere a luxuriant greenness.

The sea has, until recent years, been of little economic significance to the island. Since there are few fish in the inshore waters, the Cypriots have not become a seafaring people. Furthermore, owing to the frequency of raids and attacks by pirates in the Middle Ages, the coast has been seen as little more than a potential source of danger. With the exception of the main ports there are, in fact, no human settlements of more than a dozen or so people located on the coast.

The value of the sea as a tourist attraction is, however, now appreciated and being exploited. True, the main attraction is the 'miles of sandy beaches', ranging from the crowded and overdeveloped but beautiful beach of white sand at Famagusta to the empty stretches of the Karpas peninsula and the secluded coves on the north and south coasts. But much of the interest is derived from the variety caused by the metamorphosed rocks of the coast, hard and jagged, creating sudden wells of deep water, breaking into sharp islands. At places along the shore, too, can be found small stone chapels, just above the waterline, and surrounded by bushes of Christ-thorn. These are the places where, before the appearance of Christ or Mohammed, a goddess will have been worshipped; the original holy places of Cyprus.

THE ISLANDERS

The Cypriots are generally short, stocky, dark haired; in temperament they have much in common with other Mediterranean peoples, being strong-tempered but gentle. As individuals and towards individuals, they are honest to an exceptional degree and, above all, warm-hearted. The traveller William

Lithgow wrote in 1632 that 'the people are generally strong . . . full of hospitality to their neighbours and exceedingly affectionate to strangers'. This affection, which exceeds the normal demands of politeness or hospitality, can be confirmed by many a visitor who, sitting down to drink in a strange village, finds his coffee paid for by a total stranger. Or by the unequivocal attitude towards their former rulers: 'We fought you British, we killed you British, but we love you British.'

The Cypriot is generally not overanxious to exert himself on behalf of others—again, a typically Mediterranean condition, perhaps brought on by the extreme heat of the summer months —but happy as his own master. The island has always bred an easy-going approach to life, together with an optimism that problems somehow will always solve themselves, the general attitude being summed up by the frequently heard phrases of the Greek *Siga, Siga* (Slowly, Slowly) or Turkish *Inshallah* (As God Wills). What is destined to happen will happen; there is no reason to hurry; sleep when one feels like sleeping, work when one feels like working.

There were an estimated 630,000 people living in Cyprus in 1970, of whom 485,000 were Greek Cypriots, 115,000 Turkish Cypriots, and the remaining 30,000 British and others. These figures do not include the estimated 32,000 military personnel of the armies of Greece and Turkey, the United Kingdom and the United Nations peacekeeping force which were also in Cyprus at that time. They also exclude, of course, the many Cypriots living abroad—100,000 in the United Kingdom, and uncounted tens of thousands in other countries, principally Greece, the United States, and various Commonwealth countries including Australia.

The Greek Cypriots can be distinguished from the Turks most readily by their language, a dialect of 'pure' Greek with a small number of local words that are unknown on the mainland. (*Tsaïra*, for instance, meaning Chair, and *Angrismenos*, Angry, probably made their first appearance following the short English occupation of the island in the twelfth century.) The Greeks keep to Orthodox Christianity, very rarely marrying outside it, and never to a Moslem—the main factor that has helped to keep Greeks and Turks as separate and distinct communities in such a small island. The Turkish Cypriots are, to all intents and purposes, physically indistinguishable from the Greeks, except that a small proportion are almost black skinned, the descendants of former negro slaves.

The majority of the people still derive their livelihood from the land—a few in the mining industry, but mostly by farming. The manufacturing industry, although contributing increasingly towards the gross national product, is not highly developed and mainly serves local markets. In fact it employs a smaller labour force now than fifty years ago. The towns largely subsist on a form of bazaar economy: employment is mainly in the service sector and in small, family-owned, businesses.

Although the national economy is, to a considerable extent, dependent on various forms of foreign aid, the standard of living is high for a country officially classified as 'developing', and is rising rapidly. The per capita income in 1970 was of the order of £300 (US $750), the highest of all Middle East countries with the exception of Israel. There are, of course, differences between urban and rural standards, the cash incomes of the one being approximately double the other. But the whole island gives an appearance of general prosperity, evidenced by the number of cars in the villages, by the growth of concrete bungalows even in the remotest parts of the mountains, and by the Western style of clothes adopted by all sections of the population.

By 1970, about two-fifths of the population lived in the island's six main towns, each of which is the administrative capital of the district carrying its name. Nicosia, the capital and only inland town, accommodates almost half of the urban population, 114,000 people. The principal ports are the next largest, Limassol and Famagusta respectively having 51,000 and 42,000 people. Although each has a small harbour, Larnaca (21,000) and Paphos (12,000) are of more importance as trading centres of their districts. Kyrenia, a small and beautiful fishing port with a population of only 5,000, while also an administrative capital, for the most part depends economically upon the considerable population of tourists and retired resident expatriates.

PUBLIC ADMINISTRATION

Over the past few centuries, the administration of the island has often been divided between two completely distinct sources of power. During the greater part of the period of formal rule by the Ottoman authorities, for instance, the Cypriot Orthodox bishops held almost complete authority at a local level; between 1878 and 1914 the island, although still owned by Turkey, was administered by Britain; and, by the late 1950s, although central government was in the hands of the British, it was the underground and unofficial Greek Cypriot EOKA organisation that effectively ruled over much of the countryside. In 1960, Cyprus seemed set for a period of stability: the constitution was newly signed and Makarios had been popularly elected head of state with the acquiescence or blessing of all the participants in the military and diplomatic struggles of the preceding years. However, due to disputes between the Greek and Turkish Cypriots, the constitution was partially suspended three years later; and now yet another division of administrative responsibilities appears set to stay.

The constitution states that executive power is vested in the president of the republic, elected by universal suffrage for a five-year term of office. From 1964, however, the presidential authority was no longer recognised by the Turkish Cypriots, who had established their own 'provisional administration' under the (Turkish) vice-president of the republic.

The president appoints his own ministers from outside parliamentary ranks: those of Interior and Defence, Foreign

Affairs, Justice, Commerce and Industry, Labour and Social Insurance, Finance, Communications and Works, and Health and Education. But again, from the time of the effective division of the island, since these ministries have necessarily been more concerned with the administration of the affairs of Greek Cypriots, the Turkish community set up their own, similar, although not exactly equivalent, system of ministries.

Legislative authority rests with the House of Representatives of fifty members. Boycotted by the fifteen Turkish members since 1964, it has continued to sit with Greek representatives only. The Armenian, Maronite and Catholic communities all elect their own representatives to sit in the House, as observers only, having no voting powers.

For statistical purposes and for convenience of administration of government business, Cyprus is divided into six districts, which conform to the former Ottoman areas. Administrative duties are undertaken, as in British times, by a district officer responsible to the Minister of the Interior. At a more local level still, government is effected in the towns by municipal committees, one for the Greek, the other for the Turkish population (a division of responsibilities that was the principal source of communal disagreement in 1963). Village government is in the hands of committees presided over by *mukhtars*, village headmen.

Communal education, religious and family matters were, under the 1960 constitution, entrusted to the Greek and Turkish communal chambers. The Greek community has, however, since dispensed with its chamber, transferring its functions to the machinery of central government. The Turkish communal chamber remains operative.

Central government revenue derives mainly from taxation and import duties: direct taxes (of which the greater part are on income) give only one-quarter of the total revenue, being deliberately set at a rather low level, partly in order to stimulate business activity, and partly because of the exceptional difficulty of assessing personal incomes in the particular circumstances of Cyprus. Indirect taxes, mainly import duties, are at a generally higher level than in the United Kingdom, accounting for over two-fifths of total government revenue. Local government is largely dependent on central government grants for its income, since the property taxes and professional taxes (levied according to income on the higher paid employees in the municipal areas, but only of a few pounds per head per year) are generally insufficient to meet expenditure.

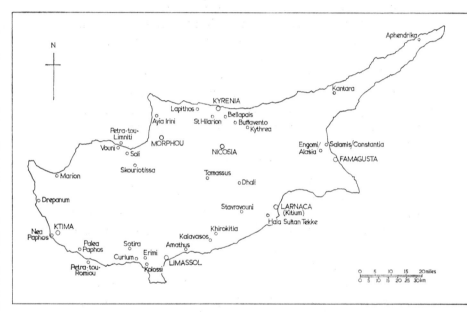

HISTORICAL SITES

2   THE GREATEST CULTURES

EIGHT thousand years of history, implanted by some of the world's greatest cultures, are preserved on this little island whose only intrinsic importance has been the possession of a few mineral reserves and its position in the highways of the sea. Yet the history of Cyprus is not one of a beneficent use of power; indeed, apart from the last fifty years, the development of the island was achieved despite, rather than because of, the presence of one or other of the great powers. After the early period of colonisation by the Mediterranean trading nations Cypriots have welcomed new rulers successively, in the hope of better times, only to have their hopes dashed and their island led into new times of war and plague, famine and depression. In the words of the modern Cypriot poet Costas Montis:

They don't know us well.
They don't know what wooden dolls in succession we are,
always down under
in an unending row,
in an inexhaustible submission,
with another doll awaiting you,
absolutely the same model, fully informed,
with exactly the same smile
you have just now destroyed,
with exactly the same gaze
you have just now destroyed.

THE EARLIEST CIVILISATIONS

The first signs of human habitation in the island date from the sixth millennium BC: this is the start of the Neolithic period, which lasted in Cyprus from about 5800 to 3000 BC. Just what neolithic man was can only be a matter for speculation: the discovery of animal skeletons and primitive tools suggests that he was agricultural rather than a hunter; he kept certain domestic animals and, as indicated by the discovery of a number of idols, probably had some kind of religious beliefs. Yet, even at this early age, he must have had some contact with the outside world: tools have been found made of obsidian, a mineral not otherwise known in Cyprus. And there are distinct similarities in pottery and types of house to those found on the mainland.

At these times the island's central plain was almost certainly too thickly wooded to be habitable; and the principal neolithic settlements have been found either on the coast, or near perennial springs in the north and south of the Troodos region. The most important of the sites which have been excavated are at Khirokitia, Sotira, Erimi and Kalavasos—but each of these represents only a relatively short period of the three thousand years of neolithic culture. Two strange exceptions to the rule are settlements on the tiny rock islands of Petra tou Limniti, a few hundred yards off the coast in the west of Morphou Bay, and the other, a shorter distance offshore from the town of Drepanum, north of Paphos. The advantages of living in such confined and inaccessible places have not yet been satisfactorily explained.

Of the excavated sites, the most interesting to both archaeologists and amateurs is the oldest, Khirokitia, some twenty miles north east of present-day Limassol. Here, on a steep mountain slope, were found several settlements, one on top of another, each representing slightly different phases of the culture. Whatever the reasons for siting a village on such a slope (and defence was presumably unnecessary at that time), the position is idyllic: overlooking the river Maroniou, the whole is surrounded by green fields dotted with olive trees. And today, as it must have been almost eight thousand years

26

ago, the scene is completed by shepherds tending their herds of orange-brown goats.

The dwellings have been partially reconstructed: round, beehive-shaped *tholoi* of baked mud on a stone foundation. Under the floors have been found the villagers' burial places— an important discovery for archaeologists. The houses themselves, built closely side by side, front on to the raised main street which runs directly up the hillside. (The most valuable discoveries at the site—stone axes, vessels and idols—have been transferred to the Cyprus Museum in Nicosia.)

The Chalcolithic period followed the Neolithic, from 3000 until 2300 BC. This age was characterised by the discovery and use of copper, the island's chief mineral resource. This, too, was the beginning of the great period of Cypriot trade, firstly with Anatolia and Egypt, later extending to other Mediterranean and eastern countries. The island grew in prosperity as a result, the population increased and new settlements were founded. The principal new towns were at Erimi, Lapithos and Kythrea, but little remains of the buildings at these sites. The Bronze Age (2300–1050 BC) brought continued prosperity; it was a time in which contacts with foreign countries increased still further. Cypriot pottery from this period has been discovered in a number of eastern Mediterranean countries, including Syria, Egypt and Greece.

The early Bronze Age was the last period until 1960 in which Cyprus was independent, although even then it did not, of course, have any real form of unitary government. By 1500 BC the island found itself in the midst of a conflict between Egypt and the rebellious states of Syria, Mesopotamia and Phoenicia. For its own safety, Cyprus was obliged to seek the protection of Tethmesis III, probably the greatest of the Egyptian pharoahs. 'Protection', which lasted until the fourteenth century BC, involved payment of tribute to Egypt in copper; but the island also benefited through cultural exchanges. Commerce increased between the two countries, evidenced by the appearance of Egyptian scarabs and other jewels in contemporary Cypriot tombs.

At this time, the principal port of Cyprus was Engomi/Alasia, about five miles north of Famagusta. The city had been founded several hundred years earlier, in the nineteenth century BC, but only grew to importance during the period of trade with Egypt when it had a population of between ten and fifteen thousand. It later suffered successively from floods, fires and earthquakes, being finally abandoned in the eleventh century BC with the silting up of the river Pedheios, on which it stood. The building foundations can still be seen on the excavated site, together with the massive city walls, some of the stone blocks of which weigh up to sixty tons.

COLONISATION

The first, and most important, colonisation of Cyprus occurred towards the end of the Bronze Age, coinciding with the disintegration of the Greek civilisation in the Aegean. The inhabitants of Mycenae left their homelands in the twelfth century BC and settled in Cyprus, later to be joined by other Greeks returning from the Trojan Wars. Bringing with them the Greek culture and the Greek language, they established the first towns on the island's east coast: the most important of these, Salamis, was founded by Teucer, son of King Telamon from the Greek island of Salamis off Piraeus. Before long, the colonists spread into other parts of Cyprus. These people were the early predecessors of the Greek Cypriots who inhabit the island today.

Some two hundred years after the Greek colonisation came the smaller trading nation of Phoenicia (present-day Lebanon), whose people also settled in Cyprus, at Kitium (Larnaca). They used the island mainly as a base for international trade, and it is for this reason that so many Cypriot goods of the period have been found in other Mediterranean lands. The Phoenician traders were later to be followed by the newly formed power of Assyria, which several times obliged the Cypriots to join in military expeditions against Egypt. Although the Egyptians eventually defeated the combined powers in 569 BC, the king of Salamis was left free to rule over the island, only paying tribute to Egypt in the form of timber for shipbuilding.

The brief period of trading prosperity was brought to an end by Persia, a growing power which, in the fourth century BC, had conquered Egypt. Cyprus thereby became part of the empire of Darius, at that time also including Phoenicia, Palestine and Syria. Cypriot military forces were put at the disposal of the Persian throne, yet the island was allowed to retain its own kings. Although, according to Herodotus, 150 Cypriot vessels joined the fleet of Xerxes in an expedition against Greece, the Persian rule cannot have been entirely welcomed by the Greek colonists; for the Cypriots several times tried to free themselves from this foreign domination. Several times, too, Greece, well aware of the island's strategic value as well as of its cultural links with the islanders, came to the assistance of Cyprus; but victory was always short. King Evagoras of Salamis managed to maintain diplomatic alliances with both Persia and Greece for many years, and then in 387 BC Artaxerxes of Persia was finally confirmed as ruler of Cyprus by the Peace of Antacides.

The archaeological site of Vouni, in the north west of Morphou Bay, dates from that period. There is no record of its ownership or use; very probably it was a palace built by one of the pro-Persian kings of Cyprus. Certainly it was a very rich building, evidenced by the hot and cold water system and the underground heating which served many of the 137 rooms. The buildings were eventually razed to the ground when their owner apparently changed his allegiance towards Greece, and the neighbouring city of Soli avenged this treachery. Regardless of the historical interest, the site itself is one of the most magnificent in Cyprus, giving extensive views across to the

Troodos and Kyrenia ranges as well as to the neolithic island site of Petra tou Limniti.

In 332 BC Persia again demanded that the Cypriot fleet should come to her assistance, this time against the Greek forces of Alexander the Great. On this occasion, however, Cyprus remained firmly on the side of the Greeks and, from the time of the Siege of Tyre, was effectively freed of Persian domination. Alexander's victory in Egypt, and the consequent liberation of the island, was the subject of great celebrations, with festivals of dance and drama organised by Nicocreon of Salamis. Yet Greek rule did not last long: after the death of Alexander and the subdivision of his empire, Cyprus was, in 318 BC, recaptured by the Satrap of Egypt. A protectorate was set up which lasted for more than two and a half centuries; an Egyptian governor-general was established in Salamis, even though Paphos was later to become the island's capital. This was a time when Alexandria was greatly influenced by Hellenistic culture, and the close cultural and commercial relationship which Egypt had with Cyprus meant that the educated islanders, too, experienced the benefits of Greek civilisation. It was during the rule of Ptolemy I that the Cypriot Zeno of Kitium founded his great school of Stoic philosophy.

Towards the beginning of the first century BC, however, the Ptolemaic dynasty had grown very weak, and an apparently minor incident brought about its collapse in Cyprus. In 58 BC the nominal king of the island, Ptolemy the Cyprian, insulted a Roman patrician. This insult was taken as an opportunity for Rome to extend its authority over the eastern Mediterranean, and the island was duly annexed by Marcus Portius Cato. Although the new Roman rulers offered Ptolemy the high priesthood of Paphos, the disgrace was too much for him and he killed himself.

ROME AND BYZANTIUM

Cyprus now became part of the imperial province of Cilicia, and later a separate senatorial province in which Roman rule lasted for some four hundred years. It was broken only for a short period when the island was given by Mark Antony to Cleopatra and her sister Arsinoe. On the succession to power of Octavian in Rome, however, the gift was revoked.

The period started harshly for Cyprus: Cato, its first governor, took most of the royal treasures from Salamis to Rome; he administered the island severely and burdened it with heavy taxation. The situation improved slightly with the governorship of the orator Marcus Tullius Cicero (51–50 BC) and again during the imperial rule of Caesar Augustus, when the finances were reorganised and money was forthcoming for substantial public works; these included the construction of roads, harbours and aqueducts. The island grew steadily richer through the export of corn and oil, wine and metals on a large scale, with Salamis becoming the commercial centre of the Levant. Tourism also became a major element in the economy when the temple of Aphrodite at Paphos became an important centre of pilgrimage for people throughout the Western world. Cypriots indeed became so prosperous later that, apparently in consequence, they earned a reputation for immorality and sloth. Their stupidity, too, was famed: Greek literature contains several references to the 'Cypriot Ox'.

In the first and second centuries AD, large numbers of Jews had fled to Cyprus as refugees from Roman persecution in Jerusalem. Many of them settled in Salamis, but persisted in armed insurrection against the Romans from there. Reprisals were taken against the Jews, the great city was destroyed and, so it was reported, a quarter of a million Cypriots were massacred. In AD 117 it was ordered that all Jews should immediately be expelled from the island; punishment for any remaining, even if they were unlucky enough to be shipwrecked off the coast, was death.

The rebuilding of Salamis was put in hand, including the great amphitheatre (which could hold 20,000 spectators) and the gymnasium, themselves standing on sites formerly occupied by Hellenistic buildings. But in AD 334–5 the city was shaken by earthquakes, the second series during the period of Roman rule. The earthquakes were followed by a tidal wave, causing equally great damage. The city was again rebuilt from AD 350, this time by the Emperor Constantine II, who put in hand the building, among other things, of the great basilica of St Epiphanios. He named the city after himself, Constantia, and established it as the metropolitan city for the whole island.

In the seventh century AD Saracen raids were to bring further destruction to Salamis-Constantia; there were more earthquakes, and the harbour was allowed to silt up. During the following centuries, power was gradually transferred to Famagusta. The stones of the old city, also, were used in the construction of the fortifications, churches and palaces of Famagusta, being removed again much later for the construction of the Suez Canal. Nevertheless, the site of Salamis—now set in a grove of mimosa, pine and eucalyptus—provides a valuable illustration of the style of Roman life in the island in the early centuries of our era. Excavations are continuing, and important new buildings are being discovered every year.

Meanwhile, Christianity had come to Cyprus, once more changing the course of its history. Two Christian missionaries, Paul and Barnabas (the latter a Cypriot from Salamis), journeyed across the island in AD 45 from Salamis to New Paphos. There they encountered the Roman pro-consul, Sergius Barnabas, and attempted to convert him to the new religion. Having aroused the anger of the local population, Paul was at first bound to a pillar and flogged—reputedly the same pillar is shown to present-day tourists—but later succeeded in his mission. Cyprus thereby became the first country in the world to have a Christian ruler. The two missionaries continued on their journeys to Asia Minor, and Barnabas later returned to become the first Bishop of the Church of Cyprus. He was martyred by the Jews of Salamis in AD 75.

Christianity spread among the people of Cyprus, being furthered by the arrival in the island of a fragment of the Holy Cross, and another said to be from the cross of the penitent thief. These relics were brought from Jerusalem in AD 324 by the mother of Constantine, and she founded a shrine for them on top of an isolated hill near Larnaca. This is now the monastery of Stavrovouni, where the articles are still held in great veneration. As befits such an important site, it is visible for many miles around, the conical, green-clad hill dominating the bare surrounding countryside.

At about this time there were some severe doctrinal differences between the various churches throughout the Roman Empire. Emperor Constantine, concerned to resolve the disputes, convened an Ecumenical Synod at Nicaea in AD 325. At this council, the Church of Cyprus, although having no great religious differences with other churches, claimed autonomy for itself. This unilateral declaration of independence was not, in fact, officially recognised until over one hundred and fifty years later: in AD 478 Archbishop Anthemios of Cyprus discovered in a tomb near Salamis the remains of Barnabas, together with a copy of the gospel according to St Matthew, written by Barnabas. The discovery so impressed the Emperor Zeno that he recognised the claims of the Cypriot church, making it autocephalous and conferring upon the archbishop the peculiar privileges which are still in force in the twentieth century—the right to wear robes of imperial purple, to carry an imperial sceptre and to sign his name in red ink.

The Byzantine Empire

It was not, however, just the church which was suffering from

33

dissension: the Roman Empire itself was divided into two parts in the year 364. Cyprus fell to the eastern half, and was to remain there under the rule of Byzantium for nearly eight hundred years. This was an empire in which the official religion was Catholic Orthodox, and in which Greek was the official language, thus acting as a stimulant to the by now native culture in the island.

But the Byzantine period was by no means a time of peace for Cyprus, since the forces of Islam were threatening from the east. Byzantium, much weakened by wars with Persia, could give little protection to its outlying provinces, and there followed three hundred years in which Cyprus was attacked by Saracen pirates time and time again. Kitium was the first city to fall, in 632, but, since the Arabs had no permanent fleet, the loss was only temporary. The island was invaded with a much greater force in 647, and was offered the usual terms of the invaders: either war or acceptance of the faith of Islam. Cyprus accepted neither, even though not strong enough for any long-term self-defence. Constantia was taken and destroyed, and more raids ensued. By the time that the forces of Byzantium had gathered sufficient strength for the relief of Cyprus, the invaders had sailed back to Alexandria with seventy ships laden with their booty.

During this particular invasion, the Arab forces were accompanied by a certain Umm Haram, a relative of the Prophet Mohammed, perhaps his aunt. Early in the fighting, she slipped from the mule that was carrying her and died instantly. As was customary, she was buried where she fell. A mosque, now known as the Hala Sultan Tekke, has been built around her tomb next to the salt lake south of Larnaca; it is the second or third most important shrine in the Moslem world. The tomb itself is enclosed within three great monoliths, although only the one stone is visible, hanging apparently without support over Umm Haram. (The other two are draped in black cloth, supposedly to make them invisible.)

34

Page 35 (above) The restored Soli Theatre, overlooking Morphou Bay from whose jetty ores are exported by the Cyprus Mines Corporation; *(below)* The Byzantine castle of St Hilarion, one of the three mountain fortresses in the Kyrenia range

Page 36 (above) The village of Pano Lefkara in the Troodos foothills; (below) Metaxas Square, the heart of modern Nicosia, capital of Cyprus, with a population of over 100,000

The island was attacked on several subsequent occasions by Moslem raiders, and agreement was finally reached whereby half of the island was ceded to the Arabs. But the agreement was soon broken, and the Arabs sought their revenge in raiding and completely destroying a number of coastal settlements. Fearful for their future safety, many of the remaining village communities moved inland. It was not until the middle of the present century, with a modest revival of the fishing industry and increased tourism that, apart from the main fortified towns of Limassol, Famagusta, Larnaca and Kyrenia, people started to move back once more to the coast.

It was as protection against the Arabs that the great Byzantine defensive castles were constructed: St Hilarion, Buffavento, Kantara and Limassol. The first three of these occupy strategic positions on the highest peaks of the Kyrenia range, so sited as to be able to communicate with one another even though up to 20 miles distant. They were first used as observation posts, later for the internment of political prisoners, and then as strongholds against the Saracen invaders. As time passed, the castles were to be modernised and enlarged for residential use of the Lusignan royal family.

Of these three castles on the Kyrenia range, the best preserved is St Hilarion, or Dieudamour, built into the mountainside above the town of Kyrenia, with a setting and architectural composition so fantastic as to make it appear out of a fairy-tale. Yet its position is so well chosen that it was never captured and, indeed, gave the Turkish Cypriots an invulnerable position in the intercommunal fighting of 1964. Kantara, on the easternmost part of the range, commands even more magnificent views, with sea to the north and south, the dwindling mystery of the Karpas peninsula to the east, and the majesty of the Kyrenia mountains on the west.

The castle of Buffavento ('Beaten by the Winds'), set 3,131ft above the sea between St Hilarion and Kantara, is the least well preserved, having been partially demolished by the Venetians.

Yet it has the most romantic history. Here, so an ancient tale runs, once lived a queen wasting away with an incurable skin disease. The queen's pet dog was similarly afflicted but was observed, from a particular time, to be slowly recovering. On the queen's instructions, her servants observed the dog's movements and discovered that it was escaping from the castle for several hours each day, going to the foot of the mountains and bathing in a small pool in the rocks. She followed its example and her disease was cured. Her gratitude was such that she founded a monastery on the site of the spring. This Byzantine monastery, Ayios Chrysostomos, is one of the finest of its kind left in the island.

The Arab-Byzantine struggle continued fitfully until 964, the year in which Cyprus, together with Crete, Cilicia and northern Syria, was finally recovered from Moslem oppression. For the next two hundred years peace reigned on the island. This was a period of great building activity, bringing the completion of many churches and monasteries. The greatest of them was the monastery of Kykko, built in about 1100, later to become the most important of the Orthodox world, and owning property as far afield as Constantinople and Russia. It was in this monastery that Archbishop Makarios received his initial training.

Following the death of the Byzantine emperor Basilios II, the empire once more declined: rebellions broke out at home and overseas, and even Cyprus twice attempted to free itself. The most far-reaching event of these troubled years was the split between the Orthodox and Latin churches, culminating in the excommunication by Rome of the Byzantine patriarch for warning his followers against the errors of the Latins. This split was later to cause great hardship to Cyprus, for the Cyprus Orthodox church was to be severely persecuted under the Latin rule of the Lusignans and Venetians.

In the eleventh century a large part of Asia Minor was still under Moslem rule and, to the discomfort of some of the Western churches, was always growing in size and strength. The Emperor Alexius Comnenus, who had established a strong government in the eastern empire, tried to free the holy city of Jerusalem from the Moslem yoke; but, unable to do this himself, called upon the pope for assistance. The First Crusade resulted, and the kingdom of Jerusalem was founded.

Meanwhile, Isaac Comnenus, nephew of the Byzantine emperor, had arrived in Cyprus with forged letters purporting to establish him as governor. No sooner had he set himself up than he revoked his allegiance to Byzantium and formed a diplomatic marriage with the daughter of the emperor of Sicily. Then, with the assistance of the Sicilian fleet, he was able to withstand Byzantine attacks, and set himself up as independent sovereign of Cyprus. His rule, one of the harshest to have been inflicted upon the island, was to last only for seven years.

RICHARD COEUR DE LION

Meanwhile, in 1187, Jerusalem had been recaptured by the Islamic forces of Saladin. The forces of Western Christendom were mustering for a further attack: the Third Crusade. While the army of the Holy Roman Emperor went overland to the aid of Guy de Lusignan who was besieging the holy city, King Philip of France and King Richard I of England, Richard Coeur de Lion, moved by sea.

Before reaching its destination, however, the English fleet was dispersed by a great storm on Good Friday, 1191; two ships were wrecked off Limassol. These two carried Joanna, sister of the king of England and dowager queen of Sicily, and Princess Berengaria of Navarre, Richard's fiancée. Isaac Comnenus, who had no great liking for the Latin kingdoms and who, in any case, had reached an agreement with Saladin, would not permit the king's entourage in Cyprus. Accordingly, he took his troops to Limassol to prevent a landing, plundered the ships and threatened their passengers. Joanna and Berengaria

39

managed to escape to sea to avoid treatment even more un-
pleasant than had already been accorded them.

At this point, however, the remainder of the English fleet
appeared on the horizon; Richard landed and occupied Limassol in revenge for the Cypriot king's treatment of his sister and
fiancée. Isaac was forced to withdraw to the mountains and,
after the arrival of further reinforcements for the Crusaders,
was obliged to agree to co-operate with Richard. But no sooner
had he accepted the English terms and returned to his own
camp than he went back on his word, calling upon Richard
and his forces to leave the island immediately. At this provoca-
tion Richard landed yet more troops, defeating those of Isaac,
who fled to Nicosia and thence to the Kyrenia mountains and
the Karpas peninsula.

No longer troubled by Isaac, Richard celebrated his marriage
to Berengaria in the castle at Limassol—the only English
coronation ever to have been held overseas. Isaac was eventually
forced to surrender at Cape Andreas, making a final condition
that he must not be bound in fetters of iron. He was taken to
Syria in chains of silver and gold, where he died in captivity
in 1195. Rebellion followed Isaac's deportation and Richard,
having no further use for the island, sold it to the knights
templar for 100,000 bezants.

The brief English rule was chronicled by the monk Neophytos in the following year thus:

> England is a country beyond Romania on the north, out of
> which a cloud of English with their sovereign, embarking
> together on large vessels called smacks, sailed towards Jeru-
> salem . . . Lo, the Englishman lands in Cyprus, and forthwith all
> run unto him! Then the king, abandoned by his people, gave
> himself also into the hands of the English. Him the English
> king bound in irons, and having seized his vast treasures and
> grievously wasted the land, sailed away to Jerusalem, leaving
> behind him ships to strip the country and to follow him.

The Templars proved to be even harsher rulers than Isaac,

THE GREATEST CULTURES

and a massive uprising was planned against them by the Cypriot people. Savage reprisals followed, but the Templars were unable to retain supremacy. They therefore asked Richard to take back the island. He agreed, although not returning the first down-payment of 40,000 bezants.

THE LUSIGNAN DYNASTY

The same year, disputes about the crown of Jerusalem had led to the deposition of Guy de Lusignan, originally from Richard's duchy of Aquitaine. As compensation for the loss of his kingdom, and in recompense for his earlier aid in the struggle against Isaac Comnenus, he was offered sovereignty over Cyprus by Richard. He died two years later as Lord of Cyprus, never having been crowned king. Since Richard did not reclaim ownership of the island, Guy was succeeded by his brother Aimery, elected by the Lusignan noblemen. Aimery was crowned in Nicosia in 1197 by the imperial chancellor, and was later to become also king of Jerusalem.

The early part of Lusignan rule in Cyprus led to a growing gulf between the rulers and the ruled: there was considerable oppression of the peasantry, and slaves were treated so badly that many of them committed suicide. Yet these first of the three hundred years of the Lusignan dynasty in the island proved to be a golden age, thanks largely to Western support for the island due to its strategic and commercial importance. Since Acre had been recaptured by Islamic forces, Famagusta had become the principal trading centre of the eastern Mediterranean. As Ludolph, a Westphalian priest, wrote,

Cyprus is the furthest of the Christian lands, so that all ships and all wares, be they what they may, and come they from what part of the sea they will, must needs come first to Cyprus, and in no way can they first pass by it, and pilgrims from every country journeying to the lands over the seas must touch at Cyprus.

Although elsewhere in the Crusader kingdoms there was considerable tolerance of native churches, external dangers and internal security were reasons, or excuses, for lack of such tolerance towards the Orthodox Church of Cyprus. Early in his reign, Aimery established a Catholic archbishopric in Nicosia, simultaneously taking over Orthodox lands and tithes in order to finance it and the three suffragen sees. The pope was also using his influence in a vain attempt to convert the Cypriots to the Roman communion. Matters came to a head when, in 1231, thirteen Greek monks refused to recognise Roman authority in doctrinal matters and were consequently martyred in Nicosia. By 1260, Pope Alexander IV felt obliged to issue the *Bulla Cypria*. The edict, although recognising the right of the Greek bishops to administer the affairs of their own church, declared the Latin archbishop to be the supreme ecclesiastical authority.

Hand in hand with the growing prosperity of the island and the furtherance of the Latin cause, came a period of intensive building activity. The cathedral of St Sophia was built in Nicosia, itself containing fragments of stone bearing Templar inscriptions, presumably from an earlier building on the same site. The great cathedral church of St Nicholas, too, was completed in Famagusta; and other cathedrals were built at Limassol and Paphos (of which little remains today in either case). Despite the official suppression of the Greek religion, many of the Byzantine churches in the smaller villages were left untouched. But the greatest achievement of the period was the construction of the Premonstratensian abbey of Bellapais on the Kyrenia range, now described as one of the finest extant examples of Gothic architecture in the Middle East. Its main buildings were constructed during the reign of Hugh III (1264–84), although the magnificent refectory and cloisters, which comprise the most impressive part of the remains, were probably added in the following century, during the reign of Hugh IV.

THE GREATEST CULTURES

The athlete of Christ

The oldest surviving son of Hugh IV succeeded to the throne in 1359 as Peter I, later to be known as 'the athlete of Christ'. His reign was the climax of the greatness of the island. Praying one day before the relic of the holy cross in Stavrovouni monastery, Peter had a vision, urging him to make war against the unbelievers, a vision happily in line with the views of Peter's mentor, the papal legate Peter Thomas. His first moves culminated in the capture of Antalya, and recognition by the emir of Alanya, both cities being important trading ports in Asia Minor. This was a satisfactory beginning, although his designs were on a grander scale. However, before they could be put into effect, Peter needed support, both moral and financial. Accordingly, in a diplomatic crusade between October 1362 and June 1365, he toured the courts of Europe—Venice, Milan, Genoa, Avignon, the Rhine towns, Paris, London, Bordeaux, Prague and Cracow. Although Peter received considerable encouragement from the crowned heads of Europe, none would commit himself personally. Nevertheless, he accumulated a fleet of 165 ships with which he sailed to Alexandria, the first city to be taken before his projected triumph of recapturing Jerusalem. His crusade proved an initial success, helped by the fact that the inhabitants of Alexandria thought at first that Peter had come to trade with them. The city was sacked and looted, his followers massacring up to 20,000 of its defenders and inhabitants. Peter's future plans were threatened, however, by the division of his co-leaders, most of whom were anxious only to return home with their booty. In the event, Peter had no alternative but to abandon his plans.

Western public opinion was not greatly impressed with the results of this expedition, and no further support was forthcoming for the Cypriot king. Their anger aroused, the Egyptians, too, began retaliatory attacks on Christian strongholds in the Middle East. Peter, in a final effort to regain support,

43

CYPRUS

sailed to Italy to plead for assistance. He met with no success and returned home to a personal tragedy. Not only had his wife, Queen Eleanor of Aragon, been unfaithful to him, but she had been maltreating one of his two favourite mistresses, the Lady Jeanne l'Aleman, attempting to induce a miscarriage of the child she was bearing—the king's child. Makhaeras, the chronicler of the period, writes of Jeanne that

> . . . they threw her on the ground and . . . brought a great marble mortar and set it upon her womb, and they pounded a measure of salt in it, to make her miscarry of the child . . . And the Queen maltreated her in many ways, with fumigations, with nettles, with evil-smelling drugs and other torments; everything prescribed by the midwife hags; and the child in her womb grew all the stronger.

(This incident is still retold in contemporary Cypriot ballads as the 'Song of Arodhaphnousa'.)

Peter was deeply hurt; he became cruel to his people and vindictive against the nobles. His severity was such that, less than three months after his return from Italy, a number of barons entered his bedchamber, discovered him lying with his other mistress, and brutally murdered him.

In response to an appeal by Queen Eleanor to the courts of Europe for reprisals against the killing, only the Genoese, who had been granted considerable privileges in the island since 1218, took any note. Rivalry between the kingdoms of Venice and Genoa provided the excuse for intervention into the domestic affairs of Cyprus. The occasion was the coronation of the young Peter II, known as Peter the Fat, in Famagusta. It was, by this time, customary at Cypriot coronations for the representative of Venice to lead the king's horse by the left rein and for the Genoese to take the right one. On this occasion, however, the Venetian took the senior position and seized the right-hand rein. A general mêlée ensued, in which the citizens of Famagusta sided with the Venetians against the despised Genoese. Retaliation followed swiftly: Genoa sent a fleet to

44

Cyprus, unsuccessfully besieged Kyrenia but captured the more important city of Famagusta. This was to be restored to the Lusignan rulers only on payment of a substantial indemnity. As a guarantee of compliance with their terms, the Genoese held as hostages the king's uncle, two of his nephews and a number of knights.

This setback to the power of the Lusignan dynasty marked the beginning of a period of decline. As a result of the continuing Genoese presence in Famagusta, trade was reduced and the fiscal system ruined. The important port of Antalya was surrendered to the Turks in 1373, and the kingdom was further weakened by internal strife. Indeed, the whole Lusignan period was marked by unrest, and, by 1426 Alexis, a Cypriot peasant, had taken on the leadership of a movement for liberation. All Greek Cypriots were united against the Franks. But the movement survived for less than a year and Alexis was eventually arrested and hanged.

Genoa was finally expelled from Cyprus in 1464, almost a hundred years after its initial occupation but, by this time, the island's former prosperity had largely vanished. The king, James II, by reason of his hostility to the Genoese, automatically received the friendship of the Venetians, their traditional enemies and main commercial rivals. He was, however, soon to be caught up in Venetian machinations. In 1468, James was married to the fifteen-year-old Catherine of Cornaro, daughter of a Venetian nobleman. The Republic of Venice, well aware of the possible advantages of such a marriage, gave to Catherine the surname Veneto, at the same time declaring her to be the 'daughter of St Mark'. For, in the unlikely eventuality of Catherine surviving both her husband and her heirs, her rights as daughter of the republic could be claimed to pass to Venice. James, in fact, died of dysentery soon after their formal marriage in Famagusta. His posthumous heir, James III, also died, in mysterious circumstances, less than two months after his birth. Catherine was thus left as ruler of Cyprus.

Much of the power was soon taken out of her hands by Venetian diplomats and she was eventually persuaded to abdicate in 1489, seventeen years later. She spent the remainder of her years in voluntary exile in the Italian town of Asolo, and the Signory of Venice thereby assumed direct responsibility for the government of Cyprus.

VENETIAN RULE

The Republic of Venice had become rich and prosperous as a result of its command of the sea in the east and the destruction of Genoese power. Even though the discovery of a new route to India had resulted in the loss of some of the monopolistic power of Venice, the republic still needed a military base in the eastern Mediterranean. Cyprus was ideal for this purpose.

The style of government of the Venetians was not particularly unfair: they retained the Lusignan code of government and the Orthodox church was left in peace. Yet, since the occupation was to serve primarily military purposes, little attention was paid to the civil administration of the island. Agriculture was neglected, marshes were allowed to form from overflowing streams, and manufacturing industry almost ceased to exist. The standard of living of the Cypriot people dropped to a very low level.

The greatest attention was paid to the defence of the island, which was systematically fortified. The great castles of Kyrenia and Famagusta were rebuilt and strengthened, although the Byzantine fortresses of St Hilarion, Buffavento and Kantara, no longer serving any useful purpose in this new age of warfare, were allowed to fall into disrepair. Nicosia was reduced in size from its previous circumference of 9 miles to a more easily defended 3 miles, and the city was completely encircled with great walls and bastions.

These fortifications were directed principally against the Turks who were themselves concerned for the safety of their pilgrim ships bound for Mecca. Under the growing Venetian threat, however, the Turks finally demanded the cession of Cyprus; and, in 1570, invaded the island with an expedition under the command of General Lala Mustapha. On reaching Larnaca, the Turks were first welcomed by the local population, glad of any opportunity to rid themselves of the oppression of the conservative Venetians. There was little resistance, too, to the Turkish advance through the countryside, and the presumed invincible Nicosia was captured after a siege lasting for only six weeks. Twenty thousand people died in the slaughter that followed the capture of the city. The remainder of the island, with the sole exception of Famagusta, surrendered to the Turks without a fight, dismayed by the example of Nicosia.

The Turkish forces did not begin their assault on Famagusta until the next spring, 1571, and the arrival of fresh reinforcements from Syria. The Venetian defence of the city was entrusted to a certain Marcantonio Bragadino, who held out against the siege for nearly four months, causing the loss of 80,000 Turkish troops. Terms for surrender were finally agreed between Turks and Venetians: included in the conditions was an assurance that the lives of the defenders would be spared and that the garrison be given safe conduct to Crete. Four days after the surrender, however, Bragadino saw fit to complain to Lala Mustapha that the local population was being badly treated, in contravention of the terms of surrender. This complaint resulted in Bragadino being flung into prison and tortured. He was forced to kiss the ground in front of Lala Mustapha's feet—a serious humiliation—and his nose and ears were cut off. Throughout these episodes, Bragadino was reported to have displayed a great courage and calmness, not once showing any anger towards his torturers. Finally, as described in 1624 by A. M. Graziani in *De Bello Cyprio*, he was 'brutally flayed alive by a Jewish hangman—a spectacle of hideous and unparalleled brutality . . . His skin, seasoned with vinegar and salt, Mustapha

47

caused to be stuffed with hay and hung at the end of a yard for a spectacle to the coasts of Syria and Egypt.'

Hostilities continued between Venice and the Turks in a desultory fashion until the republic signed a treaty with the sultan in 1573. This stated that control of Cyprus should be ceded to the Turks, and that the Venetians should refund to the Porte the costs of conquest of the island.

THE OTTOMAN EMPIRE

Thus Cyprus moved from a period of medieval splendour into the decay of a provincial Ottoman outpost. The tolerance and sympathetic rule of the Turks was initially seen as a great relief to the Cypriots since, by comparison with the previous rulers, they seemed perfect governors. The feudal system was abandoned and serfs were freed. The native population were once again permitted to buy land and transfer it to their heirs. Above all, though, the Turks re-established the freedom of worship. The supremacy of the Orthodox church was recognised and, under the Ottoman system of partial autonomy for their subject nations, the archbishop, as head of the Orthodox church, was recognised in 1660 as ethnarch, the spokesman for his community. As such, he was successful in tempering a number of potentially repressive measures introduced by the Turkish grand vizier. His authority was recognised only on the understanding that ultimate authority lay with the Turks. The Greek clergy were also given certain powers to collect taxes, an undertaking which they carried out with some enthusiasm, since this provided the means of ensuring for themselves an additional income.

There was little difference in the treatment of the native Greek population and the immigrant Turks: both were subjected to the same, increasingly burdensome, taxation; and they suffered equally from the same want of sound administration and lack of interest in economic or social development.

There was no reported enmity between the two communities, but neither was there any intermarriage. Both Greeks and Turks preserved the purity of their respective languages and respected the other's religious beliefs.

The power of the Greek church grew to such an extent that William Turner could comment in 1820 that 'Cyprus, though nominally under the authority of a Bey appointed by the Qapudan Pasha is, in fact, governed by the Greek Archbishop and his subordinate clergy'. In 1804 the Turkish population rose in revolt against the church and the practice of tax farming, but serious troubles were avoided by the intervention of members of the foreign diplomatic community.

Nevertheless, malpractice continued until the Turks considered that the church had grossly exceeded its authority. The excuse for action was the Greek War of Independence (also from Ottoman rule) of 1821: there were rumours of a rebellion in Cyprus, stimulated by *Philike Hetaira*, the society which had helped to organise the war in Greece. Archbishop Kyprianou, who had undertaken a number of good works on behalf of the Christian Cypriot community, including the foundation of a high school in Nicosia, was hanged. In addition, three bishops were beheaded; and there followed a general massacre of Christians. As before, the severity of the assault was lessened by the intervention of foreign diplomats.

Ottoman domination in Cyprus had, by the end of the eighteenth century, not only depleted the resources of the island and led to a general rundown of its few facilities but had apparently also led to a breakdown in the morale of its people. Alexander Drummond wrote in 1754:

> Though the natives were always remarkably effeminate and lazy, certain it is, they cultivated the island so as to be enriched by its produce . . . Yet by the wretched culture which it now receives from the miserable inhabitants, the earth, where any moisture is left, produces everything that is sown . . . There is not a more wanton, fiddling set of mortals upon the face of the earth.

Yet the early part of the nineteenth century witnessed a general recovery in social conditions throughout the Ottoman Empire, under the rule of Abdul Mejid I. The *Tanzimat* of 1839, for instance, guaranteed the lives and property of all Ottoman subjects, irrespective of race or religion. Tax farming was at last abolished and local judicial courts were established. The governorship of Cyprus was no longer to be sold by auction, and the nature of its possession was regularised. The standard of living of the peasants, however, who were dependent solely upon agriculture, showed little improvement.

Despite the severe underdevelopment of the island, Britain had been showing increasing interest. Her Majesty's vice-consul in Larnaca had, in 1867, prepared a report for the British Government which commented adversely on the treatment of Christians (and, incidentally, of Moslems) as a result of administrative malpractice. The opening of the Suez Canal in 1869 brought Cyprus also within Britain's military sphere of interest. Then, in 1878, to the surprise of all except for certain Cypriots who were speculating in land in the diplomatic quarters of Larnaca, the island was transferred to British administration. This occurred as an indirect result of the Russo-Turkish War: whereby Britain signed a secret agreement with the Ottoman Empire, the Convention of Defensive Alliance. This agreement had been engineered by the British prime minister, Disraeli, who, almost forty years earlier, had visited the island, writing of it as a 'land famous in all ages . . . the rosy realm of Venus, the romantic kingdom of the Crusades'. The terms of the alliance empowered Britain to occupy Cyprus and administer the affairs of the island as a guarantee against further attacks on Turkey by Russia. If Russia returned to Turkey her earlier territorial gains, then Cyprus also was to be returned to Turkey. Cyprus thus fell into the hands of its last occupying power, where it was to remain for eighty-one years.

BRITISH ADMINISTRATION

The first British officials to land in Cyprus were formally welcomed by Bishop Kyprianos, who expressed the hope that Britain would help Cyprus 'to be united with Mother Greece with which it is naturally connected'. The following eighty years were to see that hope steadily growing, fanned by nationalist propaganda and promoted by increasing resentment at yet another occupying power which appeared to increase the level of taxation without commensurate benefits to the Cypriot people.

The island was not, however, occupied for financial gain and, during the early years, the British exchequer contributed considerable sums towards the maintenance of the island and improvement of its infrastructural works. The principal cause of the island's deficit was the tribute which, under the terms of the 1878 convention, was payable to Turkey. Great Britain had undertaken to make good the difference between the island's revenue and expenditure averaged over the last five years of Ottoman rule, in order that the Turkish Government should not make a financial loss from renouncing the administration of the island. The difference was initially estimated at £92,799 (US $227,358) per year, but varying amounts were in practice debited to the revenue account until the amount was stabilised in 1910 at £50,000 (US $122,500) per year. None of the money actually went into the Turkish exchequer, however, being used instead to finance the debt on Ottoman loans on which Turkey had been defaulting since 1855.

By 1882, the British had established a rudimentary island parliament, the Legislative Council. This consisted of the high commissioner and eighteen other members—six government officials, three elected Moslems and nine elected 'non-Moslems' (a terminology which gave instant offence to the Christian Greek Cypriots). The system of taxation was rationalised and a high court was established. Considerable progress was made during the years of British rule in the way of building up the economy and modernising the island generally. Many new schools, hospitals, roads, ports and dams were built; most infectious diseases were eradicated and the locust exterminated; a policy of reafforestation was applied; the number of newspapers, free of censorship, multiplied; trade increased by 500 per cent in the first forty years of occupation.

It must be said, however, that the British administration showed little sensitivity to the island's cultural heritage, particularly in respect to buildings, either old or new. Most buildings that were erected are completely out of sympathy with local styles, from the very earliest up to the latest semi-detached suburban type houses erected in the British military bases. Nor were antiquities respected: the Turkish Government in 1892 went as far as to request that their export should be prohibited. The former Lusignan Palace in Nicosia was pulled down to make way for new government offices, and the high commissioner at one time even welcomed the news of the imminent collapse of the roof of the dormitory of Bellapais abbey on the grounds that it would make excellent road metal. Sir Harry Luke comments: 'It did not even do that; the weathered sandstone proved far too soft.'

The convention of 1878 remained in force until the entry of Turkey into World War I on the side of Germany in 1914, when Cyprus was annexed to the British crown. This annexation was later recognised by Turkey through the Treaty of Lausanne. The island was formally declared to be a crown colony in 1925, when the title of high commissioner was changed to governor. These alterations in the island's status affected the day-to-day life of the Cypriot hardly at all.

The 1914 annexation gave the opportunity for Archbishop Cyril II to declare to the high commissioner 'our satisfaction at the annexation of the island to Great Britain. For we consider this event as a stage from which it may the more easily return

Page 53 (*left*) Archbishop Makarios officiating at Ayios Neophytos monastery; (*below*) The pillar of St Paul, Paphos, in the grounds of Chrysopolitissa church, to which St Paul is reputed to have been bound and then scourged

Page 54 (*above*) Fresco painting in the chapel of Panayia Theotokos at Kakopetria; (*below*) Interior of Kykko monastery in the Troodos mountains

to the arms of its Mother Greece.' And the island was, in fact, offered to Greece at the suggestion of the French Government in 1915, on condition that Greece should enter the war to march against Bulgaria. The offer was not taken up and was withdrawn a week later.

Greek Cypriots continued increasingly to demand the right to determine their future political status, a thinly disguised call for *enosis*, union, with Greece. The movement came to a head in 1931 when widespread riots occurred and Government House in Nicosia was burnt to the ground. The rioting was stopped only by military activity on the part of the British, and by the deportation of certain leaders—a reaction that was to be emulated twenty-five years later. A sum of £30,000 was imposed as a fine on the non-Moslem population, and the Legislative Council abolished.

Repression has rarely succeeded in silencing a determined political movement. In Cyprus, demands for self-determination continued, but alongside a certain respect for Britain and the British. During World War II, for instance, although the conflict never directly threatened the island, some 30,000 Cypriots voluntarily joined the allied forces to fight in France, northern Africa and the Mediterranean area. Recruitment was no doubt helped by the slogan coined by the British, 'Fight for Greece and Freedom'. But discontent with the régime was never far below the surface and was not soothed by remarks made by members of the British Government, such as had been made earlier by Lord Passfield when he was colonial secretary— 'what Cyprus needs at present are fewer occasions for political discussions and more occasion for practical work'. Nevertheless, the hope remained that a political solution might be possible.

In 1947, Archbishop Leontios (who, incidentally, had been elected to his position with communist support) led a delegation to London, expressing the wish that the newly formed Labour Government would prove to be more amenable to Greek Cypriot demands than its predecessors had been. The

D

British Government thereupon proposed a new constitution for Cyprus, which the colonial secretary introduced by stating that 'people in the grip of nationalism are impervious to rational argument'. The British proposals were put to the Cyprus Constituent Assembly in 1948; they were rejected immediately.

3   INDEPENDENCE AND AFTER

THE year 1950 was marked by the death of the Archbishop of Cyprus, Makarios II, and by the unanimous election of his successor, the Bishop of Kitium, the thirty-seven-year-old Makarios III. This was the man who was to lead his country through the years of fighting for *enosis* with Greece to independence, thereafter to become president of the new republic.

Makarios was born as Michael Mouskos on 13 August 1913 in the village of Panayia in the district of Paphos. A shepherd boy of poor parents, living in simple conditions in the mountains, he had no formal education until he was sent to Kykko monastery at the age of thirteen. Thence he went to the Pancyprian Gymnasium in Nicosia, and on to Athens University, graduating from the School of Theology in 1942. He also read law in Athens, interrupting his studies to take up a scholarship awarded by the World Council of Churches to study theology at Boston University.

Whilst in America, he was elected Bishop of Kitium. He returned to Cyprus and was consecrated and enthroned with the title *Makarios* (Blessed). He at once took up his pastoral duties and his political career. At this time, too, he assumed the chairmanship of the Office of the Ethnarchy which was eventually to take the lead in the national struggle for self-determination. It was, indeed, at the suggestion of Makarios that the Holy Synod of the Cyprus church conducted a plebiscite, in January 1950, amongst Greek Cypriots, on their desired future for the island: 97 per cent voted in favour of union with

57

Greece. The result was, of course, disregarded by the British colonial administration.

The head of the Church of Cyprus traditionally assumes the title of Ethnarch, national leader of the Greek people of the island. Although this title is a hangover from Ottoman days, when the ethnarch was expected to represent his people formally to the ultimate authority of the state, the style continued in use. By 1950, although there was no longer any constitutional basis for this assumption of a 'national leadership', this was the role clearly preferred and adopted by Makarios III, preaching the cause of *enosis* from pulpits all over the land.

Soon after his appointment as archbishop in 1950, Makarios undertook a series of overseas tours, taking in a visit to the United States where he founded branches of an organisation known as 'Justice for Cyprus'. The primary aim of these tours was to bring the Cyprus question to the attention of the world and, in so doing, to instigate a debate on the situation in the United Nations General Assembly. The secretary-general was unsuccessfully petitioned in 1953 to include on the agenda an item on 'the application of the right of the people of Cyprus to self-determination'. But it was not until February 1954 that Makarios eventually persuaded the Greek Government in Athens to sponsor such a resolution. Cyprus was discussed by the General Assembly and, in the course of the debate, the British position was firmly restated by the minister of state for colonial affairs: following Britain's withdrawal from her Suez bases, he said, Cyprus could never become fully independent nor be allowed to determine her own future. As a result of pressures from the United States, the General Assembly did not adopt any substantive resolution at the conclusion of the debate.

A more lasting result, however, of the visits of Makarios to Athens, was the foundation in the island of the National Organisation of Cypriot Fighters, later to become famous under its Greek acronym EOKA—*Ethniki Organosis Kyprion*

Agoniston. The leadership was entrusted to George Grivas, a soldier who had risen in the 1939–45 war to the rank of lieutenant-colonel. Later, after his conduct in the Cyprus campaign, he was to be promoted to general.

EOKA

On 1 April 1955, a series of explosions throughout the island marked the start of the four-year struggle for self-determination. The first few months were relatively calm, and therefore treated with little seriousness in London: the British colonial secretary flew to Cyprus, made some conciliatory remarks and then returned home. Makarios, too, went back to Athens to demand that the Cyprus question should again be taken before the United Nations. It soon became clear that Anglo-Cypriot talks would, at this stage, bring no solution to the diametrically opposed points of view of the two sides. Terrorism gradually became a part of the island's routine and murders in full daylight became increasingly common. The Turkish Cypriot leaders began to demand publicly that terrorism should be suppressed by the authorities. Attacks were directed particularly against members of the police force, which in time achieved the intended result of causing the withdrawal of most Greek Cypriots from the force.

At the end of August 1955 the situation was sufficiently serious to warrant the Governor of Cyprus, Sir Robert Armitage, holding talks in London with Turkish representatives for the first time. This conference provoked widespread anti-Greek disturbances in Ankara, with murder and looting. It was intended to prove the determination of the Turks that Cyprus should not be united with Greece. At the same time, in Cyprus, some youths had set fire to the British Institute building, situated in Metaxas Square, the heart of Nicosia. The British Army, following protocol, asked the police if they needed assistance to control the fire; the offer of help was rejected on four occasions. The hoses of the fire-engine were cut; children poured into the Institute, setting light to everything that they could find. Every book in this, the finest library in the Middle East, was destroyed.

Eight days later, Sir Robert Armitage was replaced as Governor of Cyprus by Field-Marshal Sir John Harding. The new governor at once initiated a policy for the destruction of EOKA, for repulsing terrorism with all the force at his command. Curfews were imposed; a new armed body, the Security Forces, was set up, consisting of the army and an increasingly Turkish-manned police force; and a state of emergency was declared. Nevertheless, riots and bomb throwing continued apace; British soldiers were shot down in the streets. The cry of 'Dighenis', the nom-de-guerre of Grivas, was heard on every corner.

Meanwhile, in March 1956, Harding embarked on a series of talks with Makarios; certain concessions were made on both sides, but insufficient for agreement to be reached. The talks broke down but, before Makarios could resume his political campaigning on behalf of EOKA, he was deported to the Seychelles. He was to remain there for one year.

The governor attempted new methods of combating violence: in towns and villages where attacks had occurred, collective fines were introduced; these were imposed with some regularity. Famagusta incurred one of the most severe penalties, its citizens being fined £40,000 (US $98,000) at one time. The money payable was related to personal incomes, resulting in maxima of almost £1,000 (US $2,450) for certain of the richer families.

EOKA attacks were countered with persistent manhunts by the army in the mountains, many of which were successful in their object of capturing guerillas. Increasing numbers of EOKA suspects were detained and questioned at length, and the mandatory death sentence was introduced for a wide range of offences, from helping to make explosives to murder. On the other hand there were stories, emanating not only from EOKA

KYRENIA
o St Hilarion
o Guenyeli
NICOSIA
FAMAGUSTA
Kokkina
o Makhaeras
Monastery
LARNACA
Kophinou
PAPHOS
Ayios o
Theodoros
LIMASSOL
N

POINTS OF CONFLICT

sympathisers, of British brutality to and torture of detainees. The situation was further inflamed by the outbreak of anti-Greek riots in the Turkish quarter of Nicosia. Recruitment for EOKA continued as strongly as ever, largely relying on appeals to the patriotic sentiments of the Greek youths. This was a time when reason prevailed on neither side: schoolboys were being asked to kill for reasons that they could not fully appreciate; and, in the same vein, the British Army was reacting against violence, the rationale for which was quite incomprehensible to the ordinary soldier.

The search for a solution

In the meantime, the British Government continued to work for a political settlement by appointing Lord Radcliffe as constitutional commissioner. His ultimate recommendations were that the Greeks should be given the majority in a new assembly and in the ministries of a newly constituted state; but at the same time that the rights of the Turks should be carefully safeguarded. Internal security was to remain the responsibility of the British. These proposals were put before the British Parliament in December 1956, the colonial secretary explaining that if the Greek Cypriots continued to demand *enosis*, the Turks also would be given the right to opt for union with Turkey: partition would result.

The proposals were put to Makarios, still in exile in the Seychelles. He rejected them out of hand.

Harding's reply was to increase pressure on the guerillas. In doing so, he was aided by a new flow of information, from prisoners, from captured documents and perhaps also from ordinary people tempted by the monetary rewards offered by the administration. One of the greatest successes of the army came in March 1957, when soldiers surrounded a cave near the monastery of Makhaeras in the Troodos foothills; Grivas's second-in-command, Gregoris Afxentiou, was inside. At the army's demand, four of his lieutenants came out of the cave to surrender, but Afxentiou stayed hidden. Eventually, a box of explosives was set off at the mouth of the cave, and the guerilla's body was pulled out, burning. The incident backfired on the army, since Afxentiou thereby became a hero and a martyr for the Greek Cypriot cause. Subsequently, streets were named after him, and the cave in which he was burnt alive has become a place of pilgrimage.

Also in March, the United Nations met once again, to issue a resolution in innocuous terms to the effect that negotiations should be resumed in a new attempt to find a peaceful solution of the Cyprus problem. In answer, Grivas issued a statement that EOKA would suspend its guerilla activities only if Makarios were released. After two weeks of discussion in the British cabinet, the terms of Grivas's ultimatum were agreed. The archbishop was to be set free on condition that he should not return to Cyprus. A tanker was sent by Onassis, the Greek shipping magnate, to bring Makarios from the Seychelles to Greece.

In early October 1957, Sir John Harding resigned and was replaced as governor by Sir Hugh Foot, later Lord Caradon. Foot arrived with a reputation as a liberal and a just man and, in his early days in the island, went a long way to confirm his good name. His displays of goodwill and confidence included the release of a number of detainees from the Nicosia prisons at Christmas, and walking, unarmed and unguarded, through the streets to meet the people over whom he had been given authority.

Gradually, however, tension again grew, with increasing numbers of Cypriots being detained, and searches by the British Army becoming routine. Grivas retaliated: bombs were exploded in many public places, British goods were boycotted in the shops, and even English street-names were painted out.

In June 1958, Prime Minister Harold Macmillan put forward yet another plan for the solution of the Cyprus question: a council was to be formed, headed by the governor and representatives from Greece and Turkey, and with four Greek Cypriot and two Turkish Cypriot ministers. The departments of internal security, defence and foreign affairs would be held by the British. To no one's great surprise, the Greek Cypriot leadership had little respect for such a plan, although no comment, favourable or otherwise, was forthcoming from the Turkish side.

In the meantime, severe fighting had broken out between Greeks and Turks. It started at the village of Guenyeli, on the road between Nicosia and Kyrenia, where a party of about fifty Greek Cypriots had been arrested by the British, then driven to a Turkish area and ordered to walk home. The group was soon surrounded by Turks, and nine were killed. Fighting spread to the mixed suburb of Omorphita, from where eventually 700 Greeks were forced to flee from their homes. Inside the city of Nicosia, a demarcation line, known locally as the

Mason-Dixon line, was manned by soldiers of both sides to separate the Greek and Turkish residential areas. Foot ordered a 48-hour curfew, but even this failed to stem the flow of blood arising from the murder of Greek by Turk and vice versa. For their part, the British arrested 2,000 Greeks and 60 Turks.

Eventually, the Macmillan plan was accepted by Mr Zorlu, the Turkish premier, curiously soon after Turkey had been given a substantial amount of foreign aid by the United States. Makarios was, by now, even more firmly opposed to such a solution and, in Cyprus, the killings continued. The British Government announced that the plan would nevertheless be implemented, and that the Turkish representative would arrive in the island on 1 October. On that day, EOKA ordered a general strike, and the Turkish representative duly arrived to sit in his office ignored by all, while the disturbances continued unabated.

In November 1958, the United Nations once more debated Cyprus, and again came up with a resolution calling for efforts to reach a just settlement. Despite the bland front, talks were continuing in a more optimistic atmosphere behind scenes, with the active participation of the United States which, too, was becoming anxious to mediate between the three NATO countries. The representatives of Greece and Turkey seemed willing to find any solution. By 10 February, the premiers of the two countries, meeting in Zurich, announced that they had at last reached agreement.

Eight days later, a conference was convened in Lancaster House, London, under the chairmanship of Harold Macmillan. Greece was represented by its prime minister, Mr Karamanlis; Turkey by the foreign minister, Mr Zorlu; the Greek Cypriots by Archbishop Makarios; and the Turkish Cypriots by Dr Küchük. Although Makarios was at first reluctant to accept the proposals, his signature was eventually appended, and the basis of the constitution of the Republic of Cyprus was agreed.

INDEPENDENCE AND AFTER

THE CONSTITUTION

The twenty-seven articles of the London and Zurich agreements
(as they were later to be known) were incorporated into the
Cyprus constitution and into the three associated treaties of
Guarantee, Alliance and Establishment. According to the
constitution, the régime of the new state was to be presidential:
the president a Greek Cypriot and the vice-president a Turkish
Cypriot, each elected by their respective communities. The
vice-president was to have a veto on foreign affairs, defence
and some financial matters, and all other questions would be
decided by a majority vote in the council of ministers. There
were to be ten ministers, seven Greek and three Turkish, each
appointed by their president or vice-president. Throughout
the public services, the same proportional communal representation would be maintained: 70 per cent Greek, 30 per cent
Turkish, even though the Turks comprised less than 20 per cent
of the island's population. Of the army of 2,000 men, 40 per cent
were to be Turkish.

The popularly elected House of Representatives, likewise,
would consist of 35 Greek members and 15 Turkish. A majority
of either communal group in the House would be able to block
a measure. Thus a bill voted for by the 35 Greek members,
together with 7 Turks, with the other 8 Turks voting in opposition, would not be passed as law. Below the House would be
2 communal chambers to deal with matters of religion, education, culture and other community questions. There were to be
separate Turkish and Greek municipalities in the 5 main towns
(that is, excepting Kyrenia). There was also be to a balanced
high court; and, among other provisions, it was forbidden for
land to be taken from a member of one community for the
benefit of another.

The Treaty of Guarantee, signed by Britain, Greece, Turkey
and Cyprus, provided that the republic would undertake to

65

maintain its independence and territorial integrity. The treaty specifically forbade any further claims to union of the island with either Greece or Turkey.

The Treaty of Alliance, to which Britain was not a signatory, established that token military forces could be stationed in Cyprus: up to 950 troops from Greece and up to 600 from Turkey. They would serve to train the Cypriot Army and, at the same time, act as an incentive for the maintenance of good intercommunal relations.

Under the Treaty of Establishment, Britain was to maintain sovereignty over two areas within the republic as permanent military bases. The main air base was to be at Akrotiri, east of Limassol; the army base at Dhekelia, west of Larnaca. The remainder of the island was transferred to Cypriot sovereignty, although Britain was given certain training rights and facilities over considerable areas.

The Greeks later had this to say of the constitution:

> At the London Conference the Archbishop tried very hard to bring about a change of some of the basic provisions of the Zurich Agreement but he failed in this effort and was faced with the dilemma of either signing the Agreement as it stood or rejecting it with all the grave consequences which could have ensued . . . The proper functioning of the State was made practically impossible through a constitutional structure which was conceived at a time of tension and suspicion . . . The Constitution was looked upon by the Turkish leadership, not as a formula for harmonious integration, but as an inviolable charter of separatism.

On the other hand, the Turks maintained that

> The Constitution was both fair and workable. Its meticulously worked out provisions were designed to remove possible causes of friction between the two communities and, furthermore to establish an administrative equilibrium that would enable them to work together in their newly acquired independence. But the Greek Cypriots, who had just come out of a long and 'bloody' struggle to unite the island with Greece, were in no

INDEPENDENCE AND AFTER

mood to give a fair trial to the Constitution which specifically ruled out Enosis . . . The independence achieved through the agreements could have formed the basis of lasting peace and harmony in the island, but 'independence' was not the objective of the Greek Cypriots; they wanted to use the independent status of Cyprus to destroy the very independence itself.

INTERCOMMUNAL CONFLICTS

The first presidential elections were held, in which Archbishop Makarios was elected as president, gaining 67 per cent of the total Greek vote; and Dr Küchük as vice-president. Cyprus eventually became an independent republic on 16 August 1960. Initially, matters in the new state ran smoothly. Cyprus became a member of the British Commonwealth, and expressions of intercommunal goodwill were made on all sides. The economy of the country, described in a contemporary United Nations report as 'running along a downhill and rather bumpy road' on independence, soon began to recover, helped by renewed foreign investment and by the £30 million (US $73½ million) of British grants, loans and technical aid. Servicemen from the British military bases (the 'Sovereign Base Areas') too, were spending over £10 million (US $24½ million) each year in the island on goods and services. The commercial outlook improved and tourists from the United Kingdom and from the Middle East started to look towards Cyprus for their summer and winter holidays.

Yet by the end of 1962 it was becoming increasingly clear that the two communities could not agree on the implementation of certain fairly basic points arising from the London and Zurich agreements. The Turks were unhappy that they were not achieving the guaranteed 30 per cent representation in the public services, to which the Greeks replied that they were insufficiently qualified to do so. The Turks, too, wanted their 40 per cent of the armed forces to be in separate units; the Greeks insisted on an integrated military force. More importantly,

67

however, the Greeks had failed to permit the establishment of separate municipal councils, claiming this arrangement to be not only wasteful by the duplication of resources, but also unworkable. At the end of 1962, the Turks, jealous of their independence, stopped paying local taxes and set up their own local councils. On the other side, the Greeks in the House of Representatives failed to vote for the annual law to maintain separate municipalities, and ruled that the municipal areas would in future be administered by so-called Improvement Boards.

In April 1963 both sides took their grievances to the Constitutional Court, which held that the 'legislation' by both parties was ultra vires. At this point, according to the Turks, 'certain top ranking Greek Cypriots who had been closely associated with the EOKA terrorist campaign were secretly organising an underground army and were equipping it with guns and explosives surreptitiously imported from Greece'. Certainly, by the start of the campaign, there were at least 5,000 fully trained men in the Greek Cypriot 'secret' armies.

In such an atmosphere, Makarios presented a plan for amending the 1960 constitution, his 'Thirteen Points' of 5 December 1963. To the Turks, the least acceptable of the proposals were the abolition of the power of veto of the president and vice-president, and the abolition of the power of veto over certain bills in the House of Representatives by one or other of the two communal groups. There were also proposals to unify the municipal councils and to abandon the fixed proportional representation of the two communities in the public services.

With no attempt at negotiation, the proposals were sharply rejected on 7 December by the Turkish Foreign Ministry in Ankara on behalf of the Turkish Cypriot community. The inevitable confrontation occurred early on the morning of 21 December: an armed patrol of Greek Cypriot police stopped a group of Turks, said to have been acting suspiciously, in Hermes Street, the effective border between the Greek and Turkish

68

areas of Nicosia. The police tried to check the identity cards of the Turks. Firing broke out—it is not clear who started it—and a Turkish man and woman were killed, whilst another Turk and a Greek were wounded. Fighting soon spread around the town, and Turkish policemen left their posts in the unified force to join their compatriots in manning the barricades at the entrances to their own sector of the town.

Despite pleas for an end to the conflict made jointly by Archbishop Makarios and Dr Küchük, the fighting continued unabated. It was particularly heavy in the two northern suburbs of Nicosia, Omorphita and Trachonas, where there was a mixed population of Greeks and Turks. Makarios and Küchük together made a final, vain, appeal for peace on Christmas Eve; this was to be their last meeting.

The first peacekeeping forces

On Christmas Day, a joint statement by the British, Greek and Turkish governments called for an end to the fighting and, as a concrete proposal, suggested to Makarios that a three-power force should be created to keep the peace. This was soon agreed, by both Makarios and Küchük: the British were to control the force; a neutral zone was to be created around the Turkish quarters; and British troops should be free to move anywhere within Nicosia. Just what was to be the task of the forces was not clarified; but it shortly became evident that the entire responsibility for keeping the peace would rest on the British contingent—an unenviable position, coming as it did so soon after Britain had relinquished its role as occupying power.

One of the early achievements was the formal recognition by the principal combatants of a *cordon sanitaire* between Greeks and Turks in Nicosia. The line of the division was discussed through several all-night meetings at the end of December and eventually the boundary which had been drawn in green chalk by the British General Young was accepted. This border, soon

69

known as the Green Line, and almost coincident with the old Mason-Dixon line, was intended only as a temporary measure to inhibit fighting within Nicosia: no armed Cypriot was permitted to occupy houses overlooking it. It was, however, to become a permanent boundary between the two quarters of the town, patrolled by United Nations forces and guarded by the militia of Greek and Turkish Cypriots to prevent members of either community from crossing to the other side.

In four days of the December fighting, there were severe casualties, increased by the participation of members of the Greek and Turkish military contingents which had been stationed on the island under the Treaty of Alliance. A Turkish patient and a Turkish nurse were murdered in the Nicosia General Hospital; some 20,000 Turkish Cypriots were forced, either by the Greeks or by pressures from their own leadership, to abandon their homes. A smaller number of Greeks, too, had to leave their homes for the relative security of all-Greek areas. Omorphita, which had suffered in the pre-independence fighting, now became a ghost suburb, with its rich villas, its schools and factories abandoned to looters and to the weather.

The peacekeeping forces were unable to prevent further outbreaks of fighting. The Turks, for instance, occupied St Hilarion castle, firing down on the villages below. Severe fighting, too, broke out in Limassol in February. But the United States, concerned once more at the potential of conflict between two NATO countries, sent its Sixth Fleet to sail in the waters between Greece and Turkey, at the same time proposing that peace should be kept in the island by a NATO force. The suggestion was turned down repeatedly by Makarios. It was not until late February 1964 that all parties were agreed to take the matter before the United Nations. The Security Council met on 2 March and, two days later, resolved to set up a peacekeeping force of the United Nations to take over from the British Army.

Before the arrival of the UN troops, however, there came the

Page 71 (above) The five-domed church of St Barnabas and St Hilarion at Peristerona near Nicosia; *(below)* Traditional house in the village of Akanthou, with typical Byzantine arches

Page 72 (*left*) Woman
from Lefkara village,
famous for its lace,
where Leonardo da
Vinci is said to have
bought an altar-cloth
for the Vatican;
(*below*) In the vineyards
most of the grape-
picking is done by
women

INDEPENDENCE AND AFTER

most serious incident of the crisis to date. Turks opened fire on
the Greek quarter of Paphos, capturing 300 prisoners. Greeks
retaliated, and each side ignored the presence of British troops.
On Friday 13 March, the Turkish Government sent an ultimatum to Makarios, threatening 'unilateral action' unless there
was an immediate cease-fire. The threat was ignored by Makarios and the bluff worked, but it also served to speed the arrival
of the first UN forces. By the end of June 1964 the build-up
was complete, with contingents from Britain, Canada, Denmark
Finland, Ireland and Sweden, and with Austria contributing a
field hospital. By the end of September the British contingent
was reduced to little over 1,000 men—although this was still
the largest in a total force strength of 7,000.

By this time, both sides involved in the dispute were firmly
entrenched. Greeks and Turks were in possession of large
quantities of guns and ammunition, and were steadily obtaining
more. The direct road from Nicosia to Kyrenia had been closed
to all Greek Cypriots and each side was now confined to its own
established positions. The Greeks imposed an economic
blockade on materials of potentially strategic value to the Turks,
which included most building materials as well as clothing,
fuel and oil. The economy of the Turkish areas soon experienced
a sharp decline in consequence: but Turkish resolution was
thereby strengthened. In June, too, Grivas had returned to
Cyprus, and set about reorganising the different small groups
of Greek Cypriot fighters into a cohesive force. In doing so, he
was aided by officers of the Greek Army, despite the express
prohibitions of the London and Zurich agreements. The newly
formed National Guard thereby became more an instrument
of the Greek Army than of the government in Cyprus.

Despite the physical separation of the two sides, fighting
continued, reaching a new climax in August around Kokkina,
in the Tylliria region of north-west Cyprus. This was a major
Turkish enclave and, apart from a small area in the town of
Larnaca, the only one with access to the sea. Greek forces

surrounded the area to prevent the smuggling of arms. Inevitably, before long shots were exchanged between the shore and the Greek patrol boats, and Greek positions were in turn attacked by fighters of the mainland Turkish Air Force. A state of siege continued, and it was not until mid-September that supplies could reach the encircled Turkish zone, by means of United Nations helicopters.

The following years saw little real decrease in the tension between the two communities. The economic blockade was lifted by the Greek Cypriot Government in 1968 at the same time as the removal of a number of restrictions on the movements of Turkish Cypriots; but the Turks did not reciprocate. Soon Cyprus came to be regarded as a permanently divided island: the Turkish Cypriots had set up their own 'provisional administration' which, although strictly illegal under the constitution and therefore not officially recognised, became the main channel of communication between the Turkish community and the United Nations and other outside bodies. The Turks established their own police force and, indeed, their own separate civil service, duplicating that of the Greek Government in most respects. Children started to grow up in this new atmosphere of mutual distrust, learning to regard their fellow Cypriots as enemies.

UNFICYP

The 1945 Charter had given the United Nations authority to organise military forces in order to keep the peace in any country at the express request of its government, taking 'such action by air, sea or land forces as may be necessary'. Before the establishment of the UN force in Cyprus (UNFICYP), troops had been sent to Korea, the Congo and to Gaza-Sinai on similar missions. Although the original wording of the Charter implies that such forces would be used primarily in a military capacity, actually fighting for peace as in Korea, the role of the UN forces in Cyprus has been as observer and mediator between conflicts. Members of UNFICYP do carry weapons as a matter of course, but are permitted to use them only in a few, well-defined circumstances, and then only in self-defence. The occasions on which guns were used, or even were threatened, are very few; the troops have even been criticised for failing to do so on certain occasions.

The pale blue beret of the UN troops and the blue and white globe encircled with olive branches, symbol of the United Nations, soon became a familiar and even welcome sight in the island. It was welcomed not only because of the respect and sometimes affection that the Cypriots had for UNFICYP, but also because of the money that was spent by the peacekeeping forces—around £50 million (US $122½ million) in the period 1964 to 1970. By helping the economy so substantially, there was no doubt an additional degree of security added to the internal situation. Relations between UNFICYP troops and the Cypriot people have generally been good, and the few minor incidents to sour relations, from bad driving to involvement in smuggling weapons or people into the republic, quickly forgotten.

The United Nations Peacekeeping Force in Cyprus is divided into a number of sections: the largest is UNFICYP, in which each national force is allocated a different region under the command of the local zone commander. Attached to the headquarters is a small secretariat and a political division, whose task it is to mediate between the two sides in the many trivial disputes which arise daily. These might include, for instance, the usurpation of the water rights of one community by the other in a particular area, cutting down one another's trees, or desecrating places of worship.

Attached to UNFICYP is UNCIVPOL, a civilian police force comprised of under 200 men. Its principal task is one of liaison between the Turkish and Greek police forces—tracing missing persons (a surprisingly time-consuming job in such a small area), searching for witnesses of crimes committed in the other's territory, and similar tasks. It also carries out relatively routine observations, particularly during times of sowing or harvesting of fields in mixed Greek and Turkish areas, as well as providing the patrol for the twice daily convoy of Greek vehicles which passes along the Turkish-controlled road from Nicosia to Kyrenia.

It is, however, on UNFICYP that the greatest burden falls. Its work is perhaps best described by detailed reference to the events at Ayios Theodoros and Kophinou, the scenes of the '1967 disturbances'. These are two small, adjacent villages little more than half-way between Nicosia and Limassol. They both had a Turkish population, although Ayios Theodoros also housed a small Greek community which lived in a separate part of the same village. Kophinou was of some importance in that it stood at the junction of the Nicosia–Limassol and Larnaca–Limassol roads; but they were both poor, and the population predominantly agriculturally employed. In 1967 a new Turkish commander had been attached to the village of Kophinou, and he, contrary to the policy of the Turkish Cypriot leadership, had been interfering with both Greek and United Nations traffic along the main roads. This had led to the establishment of a (Greek) National Guard post at the nearby village of Skarinou. Some shooting incidents had occurred at the end of July 1967, during which a Greek civilian taxi had been hit; but the nearby UNFICYP (British) forces, installed in a former police station and encamped around the grounds, had intervened to prevent further fighting. Tension, however, remained high throughout the second half of 1967.

Until July it had been the practice for a patrol of the Greek police to pass twice weekly through the Turkish part of Ayios Theodoros in order to reach the Greek sector, which was at the farthest end of the village from the main road. The police sergeant was well known to the Turks, who caused him no trouble. However, for reasons of security, the patrols had to be discontinued after the July troubles, not to be resumed until

INDEPENDENCE AND AFTER

early September. The police vehicle was then prevented from returning along its normal route by a group of armed Turkish Cypriot Fighters, and forced to drive along an alternative rough track outside the village. The Turks were informed by UNFICYP that the patrols should be allowed to pass through, as they had been previously, and that the next patrol would go through the village with a UN escort. But once again the return passage was blocked and, only after strong representations to the Turkish leaders, was the road reopened.

Negotiations dragged on, involving the Government of Cyprus, the Turkish leadership and, on this occasion, Turkey's permanent representative to the United Nations. By mid-November, the patience of the Cypriot Government was exhausted and, on the morning of 14 November, the local UN commander at Kophinou was informed that two police patrols would pass through Ayios Theodoros within fifteen minutes; there was thus not sufficient time for deployment of UN troops or for the provision of a UN escort. In the event, the patrols included Grivas himself; but they were allowed through without incident. Nevertheless, the National Guard was increasing its strength in positions around the village.

The following morning, UNIFCYP was informed that yet another police patrol had already passed through the village, and, despite warnings from the UN that the action already taken was sufficient to re-establish the precedent of patrols through the Turkish sector, another patrol was sent later the same day, 15 November. This time the road was blocked; shots were fired, and the National Guard, now well established in the hills surrounding Ayios Theodoros, began to fire down on the Turkish villagers. The Greeks soon captured the village, but fighting continued, supported by armoured cars and mortar fire. By the afternoon, with fighting having spread to Kophinou, twenty-two Turkish Fighters and one Greek National Guardsman had been killed.

Throughout the conflict, the UNFICYP force commander

77

and the special representative of the UN secretary-general had been in close contact with the Cypriot Government, reporting to them the situation as observed by the local contingent. By six o'clock on the morning of 16 November, a cease-fire had been agreed, a direct consequence of the mediation of the UN and of their impartial recording of the events of the previous two days. These events, although tragic, brought about the realisation of some need for a new approach to the intercommunal differences; the result was the establishment of a series of formal talks between the two sides from June 1968, aimed at producing an agreed solution to the Cyprus question.

4   THE FAIR ISLAND

Cyprus, which lies about latitude 35°, is struck directly by the
sun, which beats fiercely on the soil and bakes it. Then the winds
sweep over the heated earth, and they get too hot, so that their
blasts merely augment the heat. It is necessary, therefore,
carefully to protect one's chest, a thing difficult to do in such
a furnace. At Cerines [Kyrenia] however the wind springs
directly from the sea, and has no time to touch the burning
soil, so that it does not add to the heat as in other parts of the
island . . . On the south too it is protected by the chain of
mountains . . . which are near enough to give the place shade
and excellent water.

THE CLIMATE

TOMMASO PORCACCHI's impressions on visiting
Cyprus in 1576 will ring true to present-day summer
holiday-makers on the island, even though some relief
from the heat is now provided by air-conditioning and iced
drinks.

The islanders' institutions, buildings, clothes and their
general tenor of life are for the most part geared to these often
oppressive midsummer conditions. Yet, taken as whole, the
climate is extremely agreeable, particularly because of the
general lack of cloud cover; the national tourist organisation
justly makes much play of the fact that Cyprus enjoys 'three
hundred and forty sunny days' each year.

The island does, in fact, experience a modified Mediterranean climate, typified by hot dry summers and mild wet
winters. Since it is in the extreme eastern corner of the
landlocked sea and surrounded by large land masses, the island

comes under pronounced continental influences. This means that many areas of low pressure are diverted northwards by the south-eastern corner of the Turkish mainland, and the island receives less rainfall in consequence than would otherwise be expected.

For such a small area, there are considerable climatic variations within the island, largely determined by elevation. Three main climatic regions can be distinguished: the central lowlands, driest and warmest; the mountain areas, with the highest rainfall and correspondingly least sunshine; and the coastal belt, experiencing an intermediate climate. Overall, with the predominant winds being westerly, the west of Cyprus has slightly lower temperatures and higher rainfall than the east. These differences mean that when corn is being harvested on the plains and even the Cypriots are beginning to swim, narcissi and peach blossom are perfuming the mountain foothills and snow may still be lying at the top of the Troodos range. Yet, from the plain to the summit of the mountains is less than one hour's drive.

Summer temperatures reach an average maximum of 97° F in Nicosia and 79° F at Troodos, 5,700ft above sea-level; they exceed 100° F in the lowlands for an average of ten days each year. These figures, of course, relate to temperatures in the shade and thus have little meaning in areas in which there is none: temperatures in direct sunshine can reach as high as 170° F. This leads to a certain lassitude among people, Cypriots and visitors, in the hottest months; but more importantly, it also has a considerably inhibiting effect upon plant life. Summer minima are around 70° F in the lowlands and 60° F in Troodos. Although these temperatures are high, they are made more bearable by a generally low level of humidity.

The average maximum and minimum temperatures in the winter are 60° F to 42° F in Nicosia (where the lowest recorded in recent years was 22° F, in 1950), and 43° F to 34° F in the Troodos area. Frost is infrequent on the plains; and, as it is therefore unexpected, it can cause considerable damage to crops when it does occur, about one winter in every two.

Although it is the sunshine which governs the Cypriot's way of life, the rainfall directly regulates his standard of living. Severe droughts can, for instance, halve the island's agricultural income and, in a country where almost half the population is directly dependent on the land, can have serious consequences. Droughts are relatively frequent: that of 1947-8 resulted in a complete failure of crops in certain areas. Yet none in recent years has equalled the severity of that recorded in the reign of Constantine in the fourth century AD, which lasted for thirty-six years or more and, according to Makhaeras, 'everything dried up, both cisterns and springs; and they deserted our most admirable Cyprus'.

'More rains, more gains,' runs the Cypriot saying. But too much rain can be as damaging as too little: crops and soils are washed away, mud houses destroyed and communications disrupted. The rainfall in this century has averaged about 19in each year—compared with some 35 to 40in in Syria and Lebanon—with nine-tenths of this fall occurring in the five winter months, from November to March. The central lowlands receive, on average, 15in or less each year, and 40in at Amiandos in the Troodos area, 4,500ft above sea-level. Nevertheless, rain falls in Nicosia on only 65 days each year, and for 141 hours (these figures averaged over four years only). Summer rainfall is generally unwelcome despite the dry soil conditions, since it is so often associated with hail and thunderstorms, damaging crops; but, in any case, evaporation is so high that the rainfall benefits the ground very little.

The Troodos mountains, too, see snow for most years, lying on the summit often until June. This is a valuable economic commodity, not only attracting tourists—for there are several modest ski-runs on Troodos—but also helping to replenish the water table. Snow falls occasionally on the plains, but has never been experienced in many coastal areas.

GEOLOGY

Some one hundred million years ago, in the pre-Upper Triassic period, the floor of the eastern Mediterranean broke under volcanic pressure, and at the same time as the formation of the Alps, Carpathian, Himalaya and Atlas mountains, masses of molten rock and lava erupted to form the Troodos and Kyrenia ranges. The lava in the central, Troodos, massif was carried with sufficient force to shake off the sedimentary layer that had been accumulating on the sea-bed; and the little remaining sediment was washed from the highest peaks by wind and rain to expose the igneous rocks full of the precious minerals—copper, pyrites, asbestos, gold—that, through the ages, have formed the wealth of Cyprus. The Kyrenia range was formed with less force, retaining a capping of limestone flanked with chalks.

Thereafter, the land mass gradually rose—marine deposits

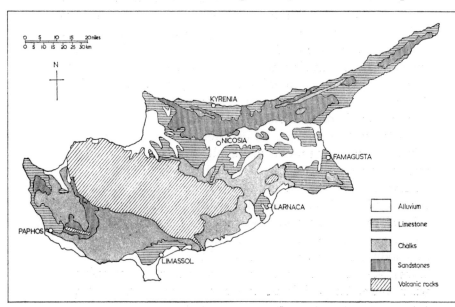

GEOLOGY

of the relatively late Pleistocene period have been found at a height of 1,000ft above the present sea-level—leaving narrow coastal terraces and a broad central lowland area. This gradual uplift of the land has left the sea around the island relatively shallow.

About one-quarter of the surface area of Cyprus is thus made up of an igneous outcrop—andesitic and pillow lavas with plutonic intrusions of serpentine. The more recent, sedimentary rocks in the remainder of the island are mainly of limestones (particularly Hilarion Limestone on the Kyrenia range), chalks (particularly the Dhali Group, running south of the Kyrenia range and in a wide band from the north west of Cyprus, round the south towards Larnaca) and marls and sands (stretching from Morphou to Famagusta across the central lowland area). The sequence of land formation has created a number of separate morphological areas, of which the most distinct are: the central massif, the Kyrenia range, the Karpas peninsula, the chalk plateaux and the central lowlands.

Geology and the settlement pattern

Of the two mountain areas, the Troodos region is predominant on account of both its area and height. Rarely lower than 2,000ft, and rising to a maximum of over 6,000ft, it encompasses a wide variety of landscapes. These range from areas of weathered rock, devoid of any vegetation, through the rounded hills of pillow lavas on the lower slopes, to extensive rocky areas dissected by deep river valleys which cut downwards in predominantly northerly and southerly directions. Soils are thin, and mostly confined to valleys. These general characteristics have determined the settlement pattern of the area: with the single exception of the tourist village of Troodos itself, villages are found only spread out along the river courses, since communications across the grain of the mountains is difficult and, in any case, there is no livelihood to be made other than where the soils are cultivable.

The Kyrenia range is scenically the more spectacular, a wall of rock out of which the white limestone peaks of the resistant Hilarion Limestone point jaggedly to the sky. It has steep, sometimes precipitous, slopes, draining generally towards the north and south. This terrain, too, does not allow for easy cultivation, other than for forestry uses; villages are therefore limited to the mountain's lower slopes, where the alluvial ground is loamy and fertile. The three passes of the range (Panagra, St Hilarion and Akanthou) mark the main fault lines.

To the east, the range drops in height to become the backbone of the Karpas peninsula, the 'panhandle' of Cyprus, but distinguished by less severe folding than in the main range. The principal outcrops here are of Kythrea Limestone. There has been considerable erosion in the western part of the Karpas, giving consequently somewhat harsh landforms; but, to the east, the more humid climate has resulted in a better vegetation cover and hence the appearance of a more gentle landscape. Soils are generally fertile and, even unirrigated, they can give good yields of certain crops. In ancient times the area was thickly populated, judging from the number of archaeological sites dating from all eras; but today, its crops declining in economic significance (particularly cotton and tobacco) and distant as it is from the main urban centres, it is a region of diminishing agricultural activity and decreasing population.

Around the central massif are the chalk plateaux, stretching from west of Larnaca around the south and west coasts to the beautiful but uninhabited Acamas peninsula in the north west. Cultivated only in river valleys and river terraces, they present a relief of rounded white hillocks, in places sharply cut by streams. On one side of the village of Phiti in the Paphos district, for instance, the ground suddenly drops 1,500ft to the bottom of the Sarama canyon whilst, on the other side, there is a drop of 900ft to the canyon of the river Ezuza. Towards the sea, the chalk plateaux fall either in dazzling white cliffs (as to the rocks of Petra tou Romiou, the birthplace of Aphrodite) or else end in scarps overlooking raised beaches. The terrain makes for difficult communications, although there is sufficient cultivable soil to have encouraged a relatively dense pattern of settlements in the valleys.

The central lowlands, which take in Morphou, Nicosia and Famagusta, have some of the best soils of the island. Although the eastern part is loosely referred to as the Mesaoria Plain, it is not strictly flat but composed of low hills, the mean height above sea-level ranging from 100 to 700ft. Large areas of the lowlands are covered by the crust of a secondary limestone, locally known as Kafkalla, which gives rise to infertile soils but which, being relatively thin and the underlying ground easily worked, was used in the Bronze Age as a natural roofing of tombs. Soils vary considerably, from the fertile Alluvial Fan Region around Morphou—a prosperous part, where much of the island's citrus fruit is grown—to the land in the region of Cape Greco, south of Famagusta, where, on higher ground, the soil has been entirely eroded away. Since most ground in the lowlands can be cultivated, and communications are easy, village and population densities are quite high.

Apart from the availability of water, one of the most pressing problems connected with land in the island is that of erosion: it has, for example, been estimated that vineyards erode at a rate of more than 8,000 cubic feet per square mile each year. That it is such a problem results from a number of causes, in the main due to the activity of man. Firstly, farming has, in the past, been carried out on sloping ground without adequate technical safeguards; secondly, the indiscriminate grazing of goats, preferring bushy vegetation and trees, has helped to destroy adequate ground cover. This has now been halted by the Goats Law which forbids their grazing in certain parts of the island, and in the mountain forests in particular. In 1926, by way of illustration, 68 per cent of the State Forests were grazed under permit (and more illegally); by 1953 only 14 per

85

cent was grazed, and the number of goats in forest land had been reduced by over 90 per cent.

The system of land tenure, as well, has resulted in there being many small plots of land, often of awkward shapes, under different management; and absentee landlords take little care of their land. Finally, the system of monoculture—practised widely—means that many areas are at times devoid of any cover, and particularly in the mountain areas after the vine season has finished. The first cloudbursts overfill the narrow river valleys and, within a short period, flooding can cause substantial erosion.

THE FORESTS

The geographer Strabo, writing in AD 23, tells us that

> Eratosthenes talks of the plains as being formerly full of wood run to riot, choken in fact with undergrowth and uncultivated. The mines were here of some little service, the trees being cut down for the melting of copper and silver; and of further help was shipbuilding, when men sailed over the seas without fear and with large fleets.

Although contemporary geographers dispute whether the central lowlands could have been as thickly afforested as Eratosthenes records, there is little doubt that forests did cover a much wider area than the present 670 square miles, and were originally composed of species of trees different from those now known in the island. The process of deafforestation was started by indiscriminate felling for industrial purposes; it continued when, due to erosion, soil cover was insufficient to support forest trees. Many trees also are destroyed by fire, either by accident (over 350 acres are lost this way each year on average) or deliberately, as happened during one or other of the armed struggles of the 1950s and 1960s. Much forest land has been cleared for cultivation (often resulting in further soil erosion) and, in addition, timber was lost for peasants' fuel until village fuel areas were officially designated. Towards the end of the

86

Ottoman period there were indeed over 300 full-time woodcutters in the Troodos forests; and charcoal was even exported to Syria and Egypt.

A French forester was employed in 1873 to report on the forestry resources of the island, but organised management was not introduced until the time of British colonial administration, which established a government Forestry Service. One of the first moves was the passing of a law in 1881 which declared that all forest and scrub land, except that in private ownership, was 'State Forest'. In 1951, a Forestry College was opened in Prodromos, for the training of students from Cyprus and abroad. Since independence, the Cyprus Government has been continuing its predecessor's policy of reafforestation, both for purposes of soil conservation, for industrial purposes (180 square miles of the forestry area are set aside for industrial timber) and for purely environmental reasons. The forests are being systematically opened up for public enjoyment, with an excellent network of gravel-surfaced roads, footpaths and well landscaped picnic parks.

Most of the forests are coniferous, although there are woods, especially in the west of the island, of the beautiful Cyprian Oak (*Quercus lusitanica*). That this tree has survived despite the suitability of its wood for joinery is probably due to the fact that, with its massive crown, it helps provide much-needed shade for animals and their keepers. Another oak endemic to the island is the evergreen *Quercus alnifolia*, the Golden Oak. This species, occurring either in pure stands or in combination with pines, is particularly attractive, having leaves of a golden green colour on one side, and yellow or brown on the other.

Another endemic, the Cyprus Cedar (*Cedrus libanotica*, subsp *brevifolia*), has almost disappeared from the island's forests. Its timber was once used for pitprops in the Roman mines of Skouriotissa, some thirty miles distant; it also suffered from being a favourite food of goats. Although under royal protection as far back as 300 BC, its slow rate of regeneration has led to its extinction in all but one area of the island, Rga Steradja. This area, known now as Cedar Valley, is in the Paphos forest, half-way between Kykko monastery and the large forestry station of Stavros-tis-Psokas. From the beginning of the British occupation, however, the cedar was once again put under official protection, and no further felling permitted; but, even so, only a few hundred specimens remain today.

The Kyrenia range is mainly afforested with the Mediterranean Cypress (*Cupressus sempervirens*), an evergreen tree with a straight growth which makes it suitable for high quality timber and for the manufacture of poles. Nine-tenths of the island's commercial forests, however, are composed of pines, two of which, the Aleppo Pine (*Pinus halepensis*, subsp *brutia*) and the Troodos Pine (*Pinus laricio*) are indigenous to Cyprus.

Although man has denuded the island of much of its tree cover, in compensation he has also brought back a number of species from abroad. These include palms, agaves and the ubiquitous eucalyptus, together with several species which have since proved their value for soil conservation: acacia, for instance, used to bind the soil on the steep gradients of the Amiandos asbestos mine; and mimosa, in the sandy soil at Salamis and in the Morphou Bay.

The most prolific trees are those cultivated for commercial crops: everywhere around human settlements can be found orchards of orange or lemon, peach or plum, almond or apricot. Because of the importance of trees to the Cypriot people in an island where shade is at a premium, many legends have grown up around them. The fig tree, for example, is regarded as a tree of evil since, if seen on waking, it is believed to bring illness and misfortune. Yet it is widely cultivated, its fruit being left to ripen on the flat roofs of the village houses.

The olive, on the other hand, is a sacred tree. There are an estimated two million of them in the island, although they grow only in places where the winter rains accumulate. Its chief value is, of course, in producing the oil that is an essential part

Page 89 (above) Grape harvest in the terraced fields of the Troodos foothills; *(below)* Grapes are loaded into panniers for transporting to the presses. Limassol and Paphos are areas noted for wines

Page 90 (*left*) The collection of oranges, for which the chief areas are Famagusta, Morphou and Phassouri, near Limassol;
(*below*) Factory showing oranges being packed for export

of the Cypriot cuisine. The other tree characteristic of the open countryside is the carob or St John's Bread, *Ceratonia siliqua*. This is an evergreen tree, incidentally a rare survivor of the Iron Age, of which there are also estimated to be two million in Cyprus, growing both wild and cultivated on even the most inhospitable soils. Although its hard wood is much in demand for winter fuel, it is grown chiefly for its seed-pods—'black gold' —themselves containing gum used for the manufacture of glue; the seeds, containing sugar, are used for cattle fodder. Their characteristic sickly-sweet smell at harvest time, once experienced, is never to be forgotten.

FLORA

As for plants and shrubs, the climate of the island inhibits the growth of most except those best able to withstand drought. The uncultivated lowland areas typically host steppe societies— grasses, mixed with low, thorny shrubs and interspersed with a few tubers and bulbs, including the asphodel, mandrake and iris. On the low-lying rocky ground there is garigue, composed of thinly separated shrubs with some herbs on the otherwise bare and stony land in between. At a higher level there is maquis vegetation, scrub land of sometimes impenetrable thickets of bushes or underdeveloped trees—olive, hawthorn and carob amongst others. Certain parts of the island, and notably the Karpas and Acamas peninsulas, have a maquis formed almost exclusively of scrub juniper.

The list of flowering plants that can be found in the island reads like a catalogue of exotic species: cyclamen and many varieties of orchid in the scrubland of the Karpas; wild narcissus and ranunculus in the plains; dwarf iris and grape hyacinth; oleander in river-beds and on beaches; squills flowering even in the height of summer; together with the herbs scenting the mountainsides—sage, rosemary, thyme.

The main season for vegetation is the early spring. One of

the first flowers to appear after the winter rains is the anemone, first white and later, as the season progresses, changing from pink and violet to red and blue. The white flowers, so legend has it, are mourning with Aphrodite for the death of her Adonis; the red ones signify his blood. The island has an estimated sixty-three endemic species out of a total sixteen hundred wild plant species, many of the more attractive species of which (the Cyprus Crocus, Cyprus Cyclamen and Cyprus Tulip in particular) are either to be found on cultivated ground or else in well-shaded mountain valleys. Of these three, the tulip is the least common, being found only in small and isolated locations—such as around Panagra (the westernmost pass of the Kyrenia range) and Dhali, the death-place of Adonis, south of Nicosia.

FAUNA

Among the animals of the island, only the Cyprus moufflon is indigenous. This is a creature descended from the wild sheep, a powerful, well-built animal with heavy, sickle-shaped horns. Occupying the high mountains up to 4,500ft in the summer months and retreating lower down to the valleys in the cold season, it thrives upon the dwarf oak. Once much more numerous than today, remains of moufflon have been discovered in neolithic settlements; and it was depicted by Roman artists on the Paphos mosaics. Wilhelm van Boldensele was one of the many medieval visitors to the island who commented on the animal:

> There are in the mountains of Cyprus wild sheep, with hair like that of goats and dogs, which are said to be found nowhere else. It is a very swift animal and its flesh is good and sweet. When I was out hunting I saw several caught by dogs, and especially by the tame leopards of Cyprus.

The leopards have now long since left the island and the numbers of moufflon, too, have become severely depleted, having been hunted with much tenacity, especially by the Lusignan noblemen. In modern times, with human civilisation being brought closer to the forests by the development of roads and of the mining industry in the mountains, the few remaining animals were put in danger of extinction. Indeed, by 1937 only fifteen specimens remained alive. A special reserve was created by the government in the Paphos forest in 1938 and game laws were passed to protect the animal. Its safety was further ensured by removing from the area all goats, and therefore also their gun-carrying goatherds. Since the elimination of the goat, the forest has thickened, giving better cover for the moufflon. There are at present a hundred or more moufflon free in the game reserve areas, together with a further twenty-seven animals (in 1970) in captivity for the purposes of breeding and zoological observation at Stavros-tis-Psokas.

Apart from the moufflon, there are few wild creatures present on the island, and these few are generally of a good disposition. Scorpions, fortunately, are rare. The snakes, against which the peasants used to wear high leather boots in protection are, except for the poisonous *coupli*, no longer a menace. And the cats, which once were kept at the monasteries of St Nicholas (Akrotiri) and Ayia Barbara (Stavrovouni) for the sole purpose of hunting snakes, are no longer needed.

Even creatures which are household names, such as foxes and hares, are rarely seen. The Cypriots have not adopted the Anglo-Saxon fondness for wild life and, in fact, tend to fear anything unfamiliar. The chameleon, for instance, has as its Greek name 'nosebiter', for it is firmly believed that, given half a chance, this creature will leap up and catch hold of a man's nose, nor will it let go until the man has seen a white donkey standing on top of one of the round clay ovens. For this reason, the chameleon is feared and, when possible, killed. Hedgehogs suffer a similar fate, since they are said to kill chickens after having had sexual intercourse with them.

Birds

Even though there are few birds actually resident in Cyprus, some 375 species have been identified in the island, belonging to 55 different families. The home birds include, among others, the jay, imperial eagle, barn owl, kestrel and crested lark. Another, indigenous to the island, is the Cyprus or Cetti's Warbler, *Sylvia melanothorax*, a beautiful little bird with a melodious voice. Many species use Cyprus as a stopping place during their transcontinental travels, usually spending a few days in the island on their journey. Others fly to the island for the winter, including cranes, redstarts, pied flycatchers and falcons; or for breeding in the summer months. Wintering birds include blackbirds, moorhens, robins and teal. Several species of heron, too, are seen in the marshy areas during migrations; storks are, however, uncommon. The roller, hoopoe, nightingale and others breed in Cyprus in the summer months, returning south to Africa at the end of the season.

The rare francolin, a sweet-singing bird unknown in Europe, has almost been exterminated, and can only be seen in a few strictly protected areas of the island. Another protected resident is the Cyprian Scops Owl (*Otus scops cyprius*). Legend relates that this owl was originally the son of a peasant family: the elder son sent his brother, Gioni, into the forest, but he was never to return. The first eventually followed, shouting his brother's name, 'Gioni, Gioni'. The goddess Diana heard his cries and, out of pity, turned him into the owl which still flies the forests, calling 'Gioni'.

Many birds confine themselves to particular areas of the island: buzzards, for instance, are seen mainly in the Akrotiri region in September; nightingales sing, although not in full song, particularly around Lapithos. The rare Audouin's Gull (*Larus audouini*), of which only two thousand are in existence, nests on the Clides Rocks off Cape Andreas, now a nature reserve area. Kingfishers are seen on the coast from time to time; and on the Kyrenia mountains are a number of Griffon

Vultures and Bonelli's Eagles. A regular visitor to the Larnaca salt lakes are the flocks of flamingos, believed to migrate from the Caspian Sea: they sit throughout the winter in the centre of the lake, a pink, unmoving cloud.

Warblers, blackcaps and chiffchaffs pass through Cyprus on their autumn migration, but large numbers of them are either shot with catapults or trapped on limed sticks. They are one of the island's luxury foods, *ambellopoullia* or *beccafico*, about which a man called Locke wrote in 1553:

> They have in the Island a certaine small bird much like unto a Wagtaile in fethers and making, these are so extreme fat that you can perceive nothing els in their bodies . . . The Cypriots take great quantities of them, and they use to pickle them with vinegar and salt and to put them in pots and send them to Venice and other places of Italy for present of great estimation.

Quite apart from these specialities, a number of the older islanders still consider that any bird is good for eating, from the common partridge to the rare but reputedly delicious bee-eater.

5   THE CYPRIOTS

WHILST it is both fair and meaningful to write of the inhabitants of Cyprus as 'Cypriots', the description is used only infrequently on the island itself, for the Cypriot people are generally classified according to their declared allegiance to either the Greek or the Turkish communities. The majority group is Greek—Greek-speaking, brought up in the Greek cultural tradition, practising the Greek Orthodox religion—comprising 77 per cent of the total population. Eighteen per cent are Turkish, speaking the language of mainland Turkey, and Moslem by belief.

The remaining 5 per cent is made up of various minority groups, principally Armenian and Maronite. Faithful to their own languages and religions, these peoples are mainly descended from those who sought asylum from the persecution of ancient tyrants of Asia Minor: the Armenians as refugees from the Seljuk invasion into old Armenia, and the Maronites from Syria. They are by now fully assimilated into the island's way of life. Both Armenian and Maronite communities have voted to stay within the socio-cultural ambit of the Greek Cypriot community, using Greek as the language of communication with the authorities and other outsiders. There are also small numbers of British, of gypsies and of other travellers resident in the island.

It is the majority Greek Cypriots (generally abbreviated in context simply to 'Greeks') who are the older established peoples. The ethnological contention is that they are directly descended from the Achaean Greeks who settled in Cyprus in the fourteenth century BC and again at the beginning of the twelfth century BC, following the Trojan Wars. This belief is supported by the evidence of contemporary Greek Cypriot dialect which, even though attracting the scorn of present-day Athenians, has undeniable Homeric origins. The retention of the original language, customs and traditions since these times has given the Greek Cypriots a permanent cultural link with Greece. Furthermore, after the introduction of Christianity to the island in AD 45 by the missionaries Paul and Barnabas, the Greek-speaking population were united to an even greater degree by their new religion; a unity which was strengthened by the grant of an independent status to the Church of Cyprus in AD 478. Today, their Hellenism and Christianity together form twin bastions against outside cultural influences.

The Turkish Cypriots, although comparatively more recent settlers, have hardly a lesser claim to rights in the island. Indeed, at one point during Ottoman rule, the number of Turks exceeded that of Greeks. Popular belief ascribes their origin to the first Ottoman expeditionary forces of 1570–1; but it is likely that no more than a few thousand settled at this time. These soldiers did indeed form small Moslem communities in the predominantly Christian island, but their numbers were increased to a substantial size only by the arrival of later immigrants. Christians, and probably Jews, were also sent over from the mainland during this early period to swell the population. The number of 'Turks' was further increased by the conversion of Christians to the faith of Islam. This drastic step was undertaken principally in order that they should escape the need for payment of the Kharadj tax, which was levied on infidels in return for continuing tolerance towards their religious beliefs and practices.

TWO COMMUNITIES

The formal distinctions between the two principal communities are today just as pronounced as if they were living on their respective mainlands. Difficulties of communication are an important factor in separating the two, although many Turks are familiar with the Greek language, and the more educated and business-minded members of both groups are fluent in English. The overriding factor that keeps Greeks and Turks apart, however, is their religious differences, and the consequent difficulty or impossibility of intermarriage. The two communities have remainded distinct and separate despite their existence side by side in the island for more than four hundred years, and despite their treatment during the last hundred years as more or less equal members of the state (even though, in fairness, it should be pointed out that each side has usually regarded the treatment given to the other as the more favourable). There has been some cultural conformance, particularly in the rural areas, by the assimilation of common customs; but the ethnic differences remain and the two continue distinguished by their language and their religion.

Separate identity has been preserved further by the retention of national enclaves in most parts of the island. In each of the five main towns (Nicosia, Limassol, Famagusta, Larnaca and Paphos) there are clearly defined Greek and Turkish quarters. These were so distinct that, in the intercommunal disturbances of the late 1950s and again in the mid-1960s, the militia and then the United Nations peacekeeping force were able to separate the two communal sectors, by means of barricades and barbed wire, with relatively little disturbance except to the few Greeks living in predominantly Turkish areas or to Turks in Greek areas. (The exceptions, such as in the mixed Nicosia suburb of Omorphita, were few but a source of great hardship.)

The physical divisions are less well defined in the rural areas, where economic bonds and social pressures for segregation are weaker than in the towns. Indeed, of the 601 villages in 1960, 101 had a mixed population of Greeks and Turks, and 112 of Turks only. Reasons of security demanded that many of the mixed villages be abandoned by one or other of the two communities during the troubles of the 1960s but, nevertheless, by 1970 there remained some 35 mixed villages, both large and small, and 105 villages with an exclusively Turkish population. Turkish villages can be found throughout the island; but they are generally concentrated in groups, partly for economic and cultural reasons and partly for self-defence. In political and strategic terms, the most important of these groups is the one north of Nicosia, covering the main road to Kyrenia but not extending as far as the coast. This area, including the important farming and commuter villages of Guenyeli and Orta Keuy, as well as the northern quarter of Nicosia, absorbed a large number of refugees after the troubles. The other principal Turkish area of military importance is that around the village of Kokkina in the Tylliria region, on the rocky and desolate north-west coast. This was the scene of much bitter fighting in 1964, and holds sad memories for both sides.

To emphasise their independence of one another and to demonstrate their allegiance to the mainland, both Greek and Turkish Cypriots are eager to display the flag of their individual 'motherland' at any kind of function, and indeed are liable to do so on almost any pretext. This is perhaps understandable on aesthetic grounds alone, since the flag of the Republic of Cyprus is a characterless composition of 'neutral design and colour' (stipulated by the London and Zurich agreements), and in any case it is rarely seen except on public buildings. Outwardly, bonds with Greece and Turkey are more important than national Cypriot patriotism. In practice, however, the Greeks and Turks have, until recent years, been very successful at coexistence on a day-to-day level. The two met at work and on a social plane as equals, as Cypriots, with little or no hostility.

There are differences, then, but since both Greek and Turk have been brought up in the same physical and economic environment, the way of life of the two is consequently similar in many respects. The remainder of this chapter, except where

99

referring to Orthodox Christian institutions, can therefore be read as applying equally to all Cypriots.

Successive periods of prosperity and famine, stability and economic misrule have caused substantial demographic fluctuations throughout the island's history. One of the most severe declines of the past two thousand years occurred in the fourth century, at a time when the population was recorded to be as much as two million, although probably closer to half a million. In AD 324 the population was decimated by a famine following a drought which, so ancient chroniclers tell us, lasted for between thirty-six and sixty years. Succeeding centuries brought more disasters, with earthquakes and the Saracen invaders continuing to keep the numbers down; and, in the latter half of the seventh century, a good part of the population, including the Greek archbishop, was deported by the Byzantine emperor Justinian to the shores of the Sea of Marmara in default of protection against Arab raids on the island. The Lusignan dynasty brought relative peace to Cyprus, with consequent stability of the population level, but the advantages of this were lost on the arrival of the Venetians. Agriculture and trade were neglected and the numbers declined from around 400,000 to 200,000 between the end of the fifteenth and the middle of the sixteenth centuries. Suriano, writing in 1514, had noted that 'of old Cyprus had 8,000 hamlets or villages, now only 800, and these in bad condition'.

The change to Turkish sovereignty in 1572 again brought only temporary relief. There was an influx of new migrants from the mainland, but the island, being treated by its rulers as little more than a useful source of revenue, was reduced to such a state of poverty that the numbers once more dropped. The first Turkish census in the early days of occupation had estimated the population at 150,000; within a few years it had dropped to only 25,000 native Cypriots. Although accurate population estimates do not exist for the main period of Ottoman rule, it is certain that Cyprus often experienced a shortage of labour, and temporary workers used to come to the island during harvest time from Syria, Asia Minor and Italy.

The British occupation brought a new lease of life, albeit not to the extent hoped for by the Cypriots. In spite of the recurrent political strife and the growing demands for *enosis* during this period, the population steadily grew as the standard of living increased, the malaria mosquito was eradicated and medical and hygienic standards improved. The first British census—the first figures that can be regarded as reasonably reliable, despite some probable underreporting of population by the village headmen—gave the total as just over 186,000 in 1871. This total doubled within sixty years and had trebled within eighty years. The most recent census to have been held, on independence, enumerated 573,000 people. The intercommunal troubles since that date have prevented the holding of another census, but the population was estimated, probably with a good degree of accuracy, at around 633,000 in 1970.

By the standards of other developing countries, the rate of natural increase of the population—the excess of births over deaths—is rather low, at 1·9 per cent per annum over the period 1960–70. This, by way of comparison, is less than half the rate in many Latin American countries. The low rate is a consequence more of a relatively small number of births—25·5 per thousand population—than of the number of deaths which, too, is as low as in most industrialised countries, at 6·8 per thousand population. These figures reflect the high level of development of medicine and hygiene, as well as cultural advance and improved educational standards.

The overall increase of the population, by contrast, has been lower than the natural increase for much of the present century because of substantial net emigration. Between 1958 and 1962, years of economic decline and political uncertainty, some 8 per cent of the total population left Cyprus, mainly to the United Kingdom, but also for Greece, Australia and other member countries of the Commonwealth. This outflow was particularly harmful to the economy, since it was largely the young and skilled workers who emigrated. But emigration, which exceeded the natural increase in the troubled years of 1963–4, has now sharply diminished, both because of the former host countries' reluctance to accept large-scale immigration and because home economic prospects now appear more promising than before. The rate of population increase stabilised in the late sixties to around 1·3 per cent per annum.

THE FAMILY

The social life of the Cypriot is centred around his family: not merely his immediate family circle of wife and children, but extending through the whole range of relations to second cousins and further. Kinship links are extensively maintained as a matter of course, and membership of a family can be a cause for particular pride. Its members are obliged by custom to give help to one another at any time and in any way possible, the help including financial assistance in times of need (and this obligation is called on particularly in relation to house-building), giving information in official dealings, lending influence in finding jobs and business contacts, and even in arranging a suitable marriage partner.

These obligations within the extended family are honoured provided that help is not given at the expense of the immediate offspring. For they always take first place, having exclusive right of inheritance from their parents. With this moral obligation, parental duties of bringing up the children are strictly respected. The education of the sons of more ambitious families is paid for to secondary and, where appropriate, to university level no matter what financial sacrifices are necessary. And girls are protected from the evils of modern life, with mothers keeping a careful watch to shield their daughters from any external male influences. Indeed, a girl who is seen in public with a boy who is not her official fiancé is compromised and may consequently find it very difficult to gain a husband—although a girl with a rich father will always attract suitors.

Within the basic family, the position of the woman is strictly circumscribed: her deportment and behaviour are expected to appear as virginal as a maiden and as matronly as a widow. Whilst the man, as the breadwinner of the family, is both permitted and expected to give full rein to his own pleasures and entertainment, the woman must remain housebound, looking after the daily chores, caring for the children, tending the garden. Her interests are home-centred and her few leisure-time activities are largely confined to watching television and visiting relatives. Much of the woman's married life will be taken up with care of her offspring, since children are born as soon as possible after marriage. Custom, indeed, demands that after each delivery the mother should stay within her doors for forty days; not so the father. The traveller Richard Pococke noted in 1743 that 'they retain here the barbarous custom of the other Eastern nations of treating their wives as servants; they wait on them at table, and never sit down with them, unless in such families as are civilised by much conversation with the Franks'. The 'barbarous custom' still survives with many families, particularly in the rural areas.

This general situation is slowly altering in the towns, however, where women are increasingly taking paid jobs—over a quarter of all women were at work in the sixties—thus gaining some degree of economic freedom. In the towns they are, in any case, better able to escape from the conventions demanded in the rural areas. Economic pressures, too, are leading to widespread attempts at family limitation, of which the church does not actively disapprove. In 1970 the average family size was 3·6 persons, compared to almost 4·0 in 1960.

Due to the stability of traditional Cypriot society, their

divorce rate is low despite the anachronistic position of women and despite the fact that, with most marriages being arranged, there are few unions of love in the Western sense. In 1969, for instance, there were over 5,000 marriages and only 147 divorces, a rate of 0·23 divorces per thousand population. The equivalent rate in Great Britain, by comparison, was 1·2.

Since most marriages are arranged by the parents, with the advice and encouragement of the close family and often with no more than the formal consent of the two partners, the father accepts responsibility for the future happiness of his daughters. Following the custom of other Mediterranean societies, this acceptance of responsibility is manifested as the dowry given to every daughter on marriage. This is, at the same time as being a simple gift, a method of passing on property from one generation to the next, with the girl initially bringing the possessions into her new family. It may also conceivably be a reason for the low divorce rate, since the wife's property remains her own after marriage.

The dowry given is generally substantial and, by now traditionally, usually includes a new house. If the father is rich and can afford for his daughter a bigger house or one in a more central position, in addition to certain household necessities and luxuries, her marriage prospects will be more favourable. This means in practice that the girl, although generally marrying within her own social class, will gain a husband with better connections and better career prospects. On the other hand, if the father cannot afford a house, the daughter is as likely as not to stay unmarried. It is something of a disgrace for a daughter to remain a spinster, so the father will tighten his belt if necessary and build one, two or more houses to improve his daughters' chances of matrimony. The more affluent parents will generally build the houses well before the daughters come to maturity, both to beat inflation and to catch better husbands; the poor may have to stretch the process of construction—sometimes the work of their own hands—over many years. The only alternative, which is not uncommon, is for parents to take the less expensive course of sending their daughters abroad to be educated, in the hope that whilst overseas they will find a husband who does not expect a dowry as a matter of course.

The expenses involved in the provision of the dowry are enormous; but the daughter always has first lien on property, and will be given a house even at the cost of the son's education. But there are never complaints; these duties are carried out with pride. The children are given a good start in life, and this is sufficient payment for the difficulties of the parents. This tradition is still very much alive in the second half of the twentieth century—helped, perhaps, by an excess of marriageable women over men in the population—and, even now, few Cypriots can afford to dismiss or ignore it.

EDUCATION

The school system is firmly divided between the two main ethnic groups, each pursuing their separate policies and each inculcating the pupils with different sets of values. The stated aim of the one side, for instance, is 'to mould an honourable and ethical character as well as free convictions enabling [schoolchildren] to develop into strong personalities, worthwhile Greeks and Christians'. Needless to say, this latter aim is not compatible with the educational principles of the Moslem Turkish Cypriots.

In the early days of Turkish rule, so far as is known, only one school existed in Cyprus. It was not until the nineteenth century that the development of the educational system was helped by the Greek Orthodox church, and by Archbishop Kyprianou in particular; their achievements included the establishment of some schools in rural areas where artisans and farmers helped with the teaching.

In 1879 the British administration had reported that 'the majority of the agricultural population have received little or no education. In many villages not a single person can read or write, and the education of the women is almost entirely neglected.' In 1911, with the spread of education, the proportion of males who could read and write had risen to 44 per cent, and of females to 14 per cent. By 1960 in the age group 17 to 24, only 2 per cent were illiterate, while in the group 60 to 69 the proportion was less than 35 per cent, and decreasing with the widespread use of government-run evening classes for illiterates.

Although the British had regarded education as a priority, secondary education was available only on a limited basis, either through private institutions or in a few communal schools. After 1960 and until 1965, education became the responsibility of the respective communal chambers. In the latter year, the Greek communal chamber was dissolved and a new Ministry of Education established. This ministry represents the interests of the Greek population exclusively at elementary and secondary levels, but is increasingly providing further education for members of both communities.

Elementary education is provided on a non-fee-paying and compulsory basis for the six years from 6 to 12 years of age. Thereafter, secondary education is voluntary—about 80 per cent of all pupils go on to secondary schools whose fee-paying pupils pay, on average, about £30 (US $73.50) each year in fees and other expenses. Secondary education follows the same general pattern as in Greece, being divided into two cycles of three years each: the first offers a general education in gymnasiums, the second a more specialised course. Additional to the forty-nine (Greek) state schools are a number of private establishments, mainly teaching in foreign languages. Of these, the English School, until 1971 subsidised by the British Govern-

Page 107 (*left*) Sheep in the mountains near Limassol—there is an increasing export trade in sheepskins; (*below*) Typical scene in lowland country, where donkeys are still a common means of transport. Here they are carrying corn

Page 108 (above) The asbestos mine at Amiandos; *(below)* A new road being constructed in the Troodos range

ment, is the largest, attended by a majority of Greek Cypriot pupils and preparing a high proportion for British universities.

There are growing pressures for the establishment of a Cyprus national university, both as a prestige project and in order to stem the flow of educated young Cypriots leaving their country permanently after studying at English, Greek and Turkish universities. Although such an institution would confer undoubted benefits on the country, it is argued that it cannot be justified, educationally or economically, with such a small home population. Nevertheless, supporters of the idea point out that the Maltese Islands, with a population of little more than half that of Cyprus, do have a thriving university with some thousand students.

Higher education in the island is offered by a number of specialist technical and vocational schools, including the Forestry College, the Hotel and Catering Institute and the School for Nursing and Midwifery. Nicosia also has a Pedagogical Academy—the teachers' training college—and the Higher Technological Institute.

HEALTH

The climate, a tradition of cleanliness and a succession of governments conscious of the need for public hygiene have all helped to make Cyprus one of the healthiest places in the world. The death rate in the 1960s was a low 6·8 per thousand population, infant mortality 26·7 per thousand live births, and maternal mortality only 0·2 per thousand total births. Mortality from infectious and parasitic diseases accounts for an average of only 1·5 per cent of all deaths.

That this has not always been so is shown by the reaction of the traveller Suriano, in 1484: 'The air is very bad, hence you never see a creature with a natural colour in his face.' Land drainage at the time was very poor and swamps were frequently encountered; fever accounted for the deaths of many Crusaders who landed near Larnaca. Malaria, too, remained a problem until this century, with every working man losing on average twelve working days each year through the disease in the 1920s. Great progress in the eradication of the anopheles mosquito was made by the International Health Division of the Rockefeller Foundation in Cyprus in 1936–7, and the mosquito has not been seen in the island since 1950.

The island is inflicted with no quarantinable disease; apart from the usual maladies of chicken-pox, diphtheria and the like, it is only echinococcosis (hydatid disease) that presents any great problem. This is carried principally by animals, and spread by stray dogs feeding at uncontrolled abattoirs. It is not an easy disease to eradicate, and a suggestion has been made in all seriousness that it might be necessary to kill all dogs in the island, whether wild, used for hunting or household pets. Echinococcosis is, however, being controlled to some degree through the government's veterinary services, supported by legislation which enables the municipal authorities to put down any stray dog.

This otherwise satisfactory state of affairs has been achieved without the benefits of a general national health service. There are public hospitals in each of the main towns, but treatment is given free only to government servants and to the very poorest section of the community, those with a certificate of poverty. Of the 500 doctors practising on the island in 1970 (which gives an overall ratio of one doctor to every 1,750 people), only 130 work in government service. Similarly, of the 170 dentists, most are in private practice. The Ministry of Health does run 21 rural health centres, and the Turkish administration runs a parallel health service; otherwise inpatient treatment must be sought at relatively expensive private clinics. And since private medical practices operate almost exclusively in the towns, the urban health service is greatly superior to anything that can be obtained by the less mobile villagers.

Apart from the general hospitals, the government also runs

four specialist hospitals: a tuberculosis hospital at Kyperounda, a leprosy hospital at Larnaca, a fever hospital at Kokkinotrimithia and a psychiatric institution at Athalassa. Patients suffering from a wide variety of ailments, ranging from arthritis and skin infections to digestive disorders, can seek treatment at the medicinal springs of Ayii Anargiri (between Paphos and Polis) and of Kalapanayiotis (on the northern slopes of Troodos). In each village the waters contain a high percentage of sulphur, suitable for both internal and external use. And for those who find such waters disagreeable, the villages of Troodos, Platres, Prodhromos and Pedhoulas are officially recommended as health resorts: due to their altitude, patients can benefit especially from the action of the sun's ultra-violet rays.

CRIME AND PUNISHMENT

In such a small island, there is little room for serious crime. Nothing will go long undetected and chances of escape are few. More importantly, honesty seems to lie deep in the soul of the Cypriot, to an extent perhaps unparalleled in Mediterranean countries. As an illustration: most car doors are left unlocked, and houses stay open to all visitors when the householder leaves. It is a matter for front-page newspaper coverage when a car is stolen. Of the 6,000 to 8,000 people found guilty in the courts each year, two-thirds are responsible for only minor traffic offences. And serious crime is on the decrease: from little under 6,000 cases in 1960 to less than 2,500 cases in 1969. The rate of detection is high, at around 60 per cent.

The island's courts may inflict eight types of punishment on offenders: death, imprisonment, flogging, whipping, fining, payment of compensation, binding over to keep the peace and binding over to come up for judgement or supervision. Flogging and whipping have not, however, been used since the establishment of the republic; and, following international opinion, the death sentence has not been applied since 1962.

Imprisonment is served in the Nicosia Central Prisons, and young people under eighteen years old can be committed to the Lambousa Reformatory School.

The Cypriot judicial system is composed of a mixture of constitutional law, common law based on Ottoman and English precedent, and public law; additionally, there are ecclesiastical tribunals of the five main religious groups (Greek Orthodox, Muslim, Armenian, Maronite and Catholic), which have total jurisdiction over the matters of marriage, divorce and other family relations of members of their churches. The overall concept of the system is otherwise not unlike that of the United Kingdom, with the striking exception that there is no trial by jury—for it would be difficult to find an unbiased jury with no family or other ties with an accused person.

RECREATION AND LEISURE

The island has strong athletic traditions, dating from the time of its original Hellenisation: well-preserved gymnasiums have been discovered and partially reconstructed at Salamis and Curium. Cypriot gymnasts, too, are reported to have participated in the early Olympic Games, in which only free-born Greeks were allowed to take part. There are even two recorded instances of Cypriots winning first places at the Games. The athletic tradition continued until the time of the Turkish occupation when, although weightlifting was encouraged as the national sport, athletics as such were not greatly emphasised. It was not until the British period, when physical education became a part of the school curriculum, that the revival started, with Cypriot athletes attending the first of the modern series of Olympic Games in Athens in 1896. There are now several major athletic meetings organised each year, held both in the towns and in village athletic grounds.

Active recreation plays an important part in the lives of most Cypriots, football being by far the most popular sport. This game attracts more spectators than any other, and in all parts of the island. The Cyprus Football Association, established in 1834, administers the thirty-six teams in the three league divisions. Cyprus also takes part in the European Cup and World Cup matches played, when at home, in the Nicosia Stadium. Although, as would be expected from such a small country, the teams rarely win any of these international matches, they always carry themselves with distinction.

Most other sports are represented on the island, and there are individual clubs for tennis, flying, horse racing, motor sports, basketball and clay-pigeon shooting amongst others. Skiing is practised by a handful of enthusiasts for a few weeks each year on Mount Olympus, where the ski club offers two ski-lifts, a shelter and a shop for hiring and selling equipment. There are long-term plans for improving the facilities here, in the hope of attracting a greater number of tourists, particularly from neighbouring Middle East countries, for the skiing season. The greater part of the support for these minority sports, however, derives from the foreigners on the island and little, as yet, from the Cypriots themselves. Sea sports, too, have a surprisingly small following from a people who all live within twenty-five miles of the coast. Water-skiing, sailing and aqua-lung diving are all in evidence, but their popularity is limited.

As in many other Mediterranean countries, game shooting enjoys great popularity, with over 30,000 licences issued annually; the aim of the exercise is merely to bring in as big a bag as possible of any kind of bird. The sport is practised with much enthusiasm, but often with little expertise: anything that flies is fit to be shot—and if it can be done without leaving the car, so much the better. The Smithsonian Institution of the United States has estimated that around 10 million birds are killed in Cyprus each year (an average of more than fifteen birds for every man, woman and child), by shooting, trapping and liming. Some limitations on hunting are imposed by the government in that certain birds are officially protected (even though some birds on the list are now extinct), and by the restriction of shooting to certain days in the winter months. Game reserves have also been demarcated throughout the island. These are, however, not altogether effective since, as the areas often contain no fresh water, the birds will fly out of the restricted zone and into the sights of the guns of the waiting hunters.

The cinema is an important source of entertainment, in the larger villages as much as in the main urban centres—around one hundred villages can boast of a cinema. The local taste in films tends to reflect the eastern temperament, orientated mainly towards American-produced westerns and other stories of love and violence, with a slight admixture of the more innocuous Greek and Turkish films. Since most films reach Cyprus as part of the Middle East circuit, they are subtitled in French and Arabic as well as in Greek or Turkish. Unfortunately for sensation-seekers, they are also severely cut at times to suit Arab tastes and sensibilities—and to slot the film and advertisements into a two-hour programme.

In towns, the cinema is supplemented with night-clubs and cabarets, frequented by adult men of all classes as well as by women of the higher socio-economic groups. Certain entertainment centres, however, and notably Nicosia's Regina Street, a night-time oasis of light, noise and exuberant laughter, surrounded by the dark and narrow streets of the old town, are carefully avoided by all respectable Cypriot women.

But despite the proliferation of sports clubs and entertainment facilities, it is little exaggeration to say that the principal spare-time occupation of the average Cypriot man, be he Greek, Turk, Armenian or Maronite, is sitting. Sitting, discussing the vanity of the world, money, politics, smoking a hubble-bubble (drugs are severely prohibited); or simply sitting, not drinking, not talking, just contemplating the world going by.

The focal meeting places are the *kapheneia*, coffee shops, where next to the long-bearded priest will sit the merchant in his best suit and the peasant, dressed in *vrachas*, the traditional baggy trousers, leaning on his tall wooden stick. These coffee shops are as much a part of the life of the island as pubs are in England, and equally difficult to compare with any other institution. Predominantly, of course, they are places for drinking coffee. They are also, in most parts of the island, the only places for meeting friends and exchanging gossip, a source of information as well as acting as the local poste restante. The sizes and styles of the coffee shops vary little: invariably they are furnished with a few simple rush-seated chairs, which serve also as tables, standing outside the building in the village square under an old tree, even in winter. Their décor may be scruffy, but the warmth and friendliness of the atmosphere is truly Cypriot.

One of the more popular ways of spending a Sunday is for the whole family to retire to the coast or to the countryside in order to eat their kebabs under an olive tree or near to a shrine. The meal, like everything else in the island, is never a hurried affair, and provides an opportunity to drink and talk at leisure. On days of festivity, whether they be religious holidays, one for celebrating a family event such as a name day, or on an even more tenuous excuse, the family will gather for a more extended meal. This is often *klephtiko*, cooked in the thieves' way. A fire is lit inside one of the beehive-shaped clay ovens in the open air; when the flames die down, the embers are covered with green leaves, the meat placed on top of the leaves and the oven then sealed for a period of some hours until the meat is cooked. This meat—mutton or goat—is then eaten with bread and a raw vegetable salad, liberally washed down with beer and brandy (wine is for more everyday consumption).

LEGEND AND TRADITION

Many of the main customs of the island are either closely connected with Christian traditions or else have been translated

from the original pagan rites into occasions of religious significance. The most famous of all legends connected with Cyprus
is that of Aphrodite, Goddess of Love. The origins of the legend
are doubtful, although Lilio, writing in 1551, put forward one
explanation, 'that the women are very lustful, and so we read
in Justin that Cypriot girls before they marry are wont to lend
themselves to the unholy pleasures of foreigners who touch there
in ships, so that our ancestors were not without reason in saying
that the island was sacred to Venus'. But, regardless of the
historical background, the celebration of Aphrodite rising from
the waves is still held. As a pagan festival this once made Paphos
into one of the most renowned cities of the Hellenistic world;
and it is now incorporated into the Christian calendar. Today
celebrated as Cataclysmos, fifty days after the Orthodox
Easter, itself one week after the Catholic Easter, this is an
island-wide sea festival, also suggested as having been a
commemoration of the great flood of Noah. No longer does
Aphrodite herself appear naked over the waves, but there are
opportunities for great celebrations, particularly in Larnaca,
with sea sports, competitions and various carnivals.

Other absorptions into the modern Christian traditions (and
hence from which the Turkish Cypriots stand aloof) include
the use of waxen effigies as offerings to saints for the cure of
afflictions. Many churches are piled high with now-abandoned
wax legs, hearts, breasts and other limbs and organs. Similarly,
a number of former pagan shrines have been taken over for
contemporary use. In and around these places, often simple
caves, can always be seen numerous rags torn from complain-
ants' garments, offerings to the appropriate saint.

A catalogue of the customs of the island would be tedious;
but so strongly is tradition a part of the everyday life of the
Cypriots that mention must be made of the story of Dighenis,
which has again taken root in modern Cyprus. The legendary
hero was in love with a certain queen of the island, known in
tale simply as 'Regina'. He was jilted and, in taking his revenge,

116

hurled a large rock from the mountains at the queen's palace in Paphos. The rock missed, but stands today at the entrance to the town. The same Dighenis is known also as having thrown rocks at the Saracen invaders from the heights of the Kyrenia mountains; and the prominent rock group of Pentadactylos is said to have been thrown by him. His name remains in Cypriot lore as does Grivas', leader of the EOKA fighters.

The Wedding

One particular feature of Cypriot life that has taken on a traditional aspect is the village wedding ceremony. The whole village is invited to the celebrations, together with all the relatives of the two families, a good number of friends from farther distant, and any other visitor who would like to attend. The junketings, which used to last for three days with a predetermined order of events, are now shortened to one or two days, but few of the old customs have been discarded. Many small points of protocol must be correctly observed before marriage: the ceremony of filling the mattress, undertaken with accompanying dances, the blessing of the bride by her father, and the ceremonious shaving of the groom, among others; the details vary slightly from district to district.

The church service is held on a Sunday, any other day being considered unlucky. In church, bride and groom are attended by their bridesmaids and best men—the number of each is determined by the amount of money they can afford to pay towards the priest's services. Their duties, apart from post-marital care of the couple with financial assistance, advice, even physical protection at times, is to exchange rings during the service and to sign the ribbons attached to the couple's headdresses. The principal best man and the chief bridesmaid will later become godparents of the couple's first child. They thereby enter into a virtual blood relationship, since their children are legally prohibited from marrying their godchildren.

Guests are invited into the new home immediately after the

church service and are shown around each room. After giving their presents to the married couple, the guests retire outside the house to receive, from the best men, a glass of brandy and a piece of seed cake. Then begins the feasting at rows of tables set out in the garden or in the street: goat, chicken, lamb, hot from the oven, roast potatoes and salad, with quantities of beer and brandy. During the meal and later there will be dancing to a band of accordion, violin and drums. At this point, guests witness the dance of the young couple, during which paper money is pinned on to their clothes until completely covered.

Although once a major part of the ceremony, contemporary sensibilities have dictated that consummation of the marriage is now only rarely celebrated, whether by firing guns or by the display of the wedding sheet from a bedroom window.

THE ARTS

The most important and popular of the arts of Cyprus are its music and dance which, due to the island's geographical and cultural isolation, have changed little over the centuries. Certain melodies, for instance, have been retained in a particularly primitive form and the structure of the music reveals the survival of a number of ancient Greek modes. In its purest form, the music is played on shepherds' flutes (*auloi*); for performance, traditionally by a duo of violin and lute (*bouzouki*). Dances are generally performed now only on special occasions, notably weddings, by pairs of men or of women; the men's dances are the more lively whereas those of the women are more delicate and restrained. Many dances, too, can be traced back to very ancient origins; the dance of the knife is probably derived from the Pyrrhic war dance.

Poetry and song are a part of the islander's way of life: poetry is the subject, too, of competitions at many of the annual fairs and festivals, and during Cataclysmos in particular. These *chatismata*, attended by hundreds of people for hours on end, consist of a dialogue between the two contestants, *pietarides*, in rhyming couplets, sometimes scurrilous, often trivial, but always entertaining. One of the more endearing features of the island's poetry is its appeal to the man in the street—written by the uneducated, often published by themselves and sold in sheet form in coffee shops and on street-corners for a few coins. Although few of the pieces can claim literary merit, many— ballads about famous heroes or else about specific activities like sowing and harvesting—are passed down in song from generation to generation.

Music and dance may then be part of the national heritage, but the Cypriots have attained little international recognition within any of the major arts. Indeed, the only artistic form which has really developed beyond purely traditional lines is painting. Apart from religious paintings of frescoes and ikons, which is practised even today in several monasteries, the style is significantly individual. One particular artist whose name is well known outside the island is Michael Kasiolos, a primitive painter still living in his oil-lit home in the Troodos mountains. A number of other Cypriot artists have exhibited abroad without, however, having achieved true fame.

Local literature, too, is not well established—the Cypriot dialect is sufficiently different from the language of the mainland to prevent the marketing of books overseas on any worthwhile scale. And, in contrast to the Greek mainland, the theatre has, until recent years, rarely been represented on the island other than by visiting companies. This, however, is not for want of suitable premises: apart from the grand Roman amphitheatres of Salamis, Curium and Soli, Nicosia has a very fine modern, albeit rarely used, municipal theatre. In 1971, however, a Cyprus Theatre Organisation was established to present classical and modern plays in Greek. Performances take place on the basis of an alternating repertory in all the towns and major agricultural centres.

The relative lack of artistic development in Cyprus is perhaps due to the limited market, both in its absolute size and in terms of the appreciation of art by a rural public that was brought up under foreign régimes which, at best, did not encourage local cultural expression. Furthermore, as Attalides comments, 'the pre-eminence of the ethnic conflict in Cyprus . . . is not conducive to autonomous cultural development . . . as the overt symbolism makes [works of art] particularly liable to political interpretation'. Nevertheless, the government as well as the Greek and Turkish local authorities is successfully promoting a greater appreciation of the arts by, for example, the establishment of the national theatre company, the organisation of an annual pancyprian art exhibition and financial assistance to artistic, literary and other cultural associations.

6   THE ECONOMY

CYPRUS is an agricultural nation and a developing country. However, with a per capita income exceeding that of most of its eastern Mediterranean neighbours, with unemployment averaging 1 per cent or less throughout the late 1960s and early 1970s, with no real problems of poverty and with a consistent surplus in the balance of payments, the surface picture is of a very healthy economy. This picture is, nevertheless, highly misleading. A statement by the financial secretary to the colonial government in 1957 is largely valid today:

> [The problem is] the extent to which the Cyprus economy, and the standards of living enjoyed by its people, are now dependent on mineral resources and its invisible exports. The former are wasting assets and the latter must diminish as the Service Departments complete their programmes. The problem of the future is to develop new sources of wealth to enable existing standards to be improved for an increasing population.

Before World War II, the economy of the island was basically self-sufficient, with the majority of the people dependent on agriculture for their livelihood. The post-war period brought fresh investments with the island's revived importance as a military base and because of a rapid increase in the value of its minerals. A further substantial stimulus to the economy was provided by the Korean War and its effects on mineral prices, as well as by a greatly increased British military presence in the island. The latter was the result of troops being moved from the newly independent India and Pakistan and because of the creation of Israel and the loss of the bases in Egypt. The island's wealth grew accordingly, and with it a need for greater exports.

The main problem of the 1960s, then, was that the value of imports was consistently double that of exports. (The United Kingdom was the main trading partner, providing one-third of all imports and taking nearly half of the exports, principally agricultural produce and minerals.) That there was also a surplus in the balance of payments was due to the level of invisible earnings which, in turn, were largely composed of expenditure by the foreign military forces on the island. These massive drafts of indirect foreign aid have been, in fact, equivalent to as much as 15 per cent of the total national income.

The growth of the internal economy has been restrained by continuing intercommunal stresses; and full employment (albeit accompanied by widespread underemployment) has brought in its wake the usual industrial disputes. In attempting to right these basic instabilities in the economy, the government has been directing its efforts since independence towards increasing agricultural production and stimulating the movement towards greater industrialisation. The principal pivot for these efforts has been the five-year national economic development plans; but since most of the economy is in private hands, these plans can be no more than indicative. Indeed, the government's general policy as stated in the report on the Second Five-Year Plan is that 'too much control and licensing would stifle private initiative and might lead to inefficiency'. Yet despite the progress of modernisation initiated during the British colonial period, and the undeniable economic progress made since 1960, the country's free-enterprise economy is rooted in tradition; and the natural conservatism of the Cypriot is making the necessary transition to a modern economy difficult to achieve.

MINING

The name of the island, *Kypros*, is said to derive from the principal item of commerce of the Bronze Age—copper. Copper implements played a vital part in the life of the early inhabitants; the metal became a major item of trade, one of the prizes of ownership of the island, and it has been partly responsible for the continued importance of Cyprus in international relations and for the intermixture of cultural influences. Phoenician copper workings have been tentatively identified at various locations, and there are extensive remains of the Roman workings at Skouriotissa ('Our Lady of the Slag Heaps') south of Xeros in Morphou Bay. In subsequent centuries, however, the mining of this mineral was neglected, and it was not until World War I and the consequent rise in prices that any mines were reopened—on this occasion, just as they had been twenty-seven centuries earlier, with the aid of foreign capital. In the inter-war period, copper became once more the principal export and still more mines were reopened in a number of places in the Troodos foothills, bringing much-needed employment to these agriculturally poor areas. By the beginning of the 1960s, however, the resources had become severely depleted and, despite a continuing high level of world demand, a number of mines were closed down. By the end of the sixties, total copper production, all of which is exported in its unmanufactured form, was less than one-third of the quantity thirty years earlier.

Copper pyrites is mined, either open-cast or underground (the Mavrovouni mine, Lefka, is worked at 300ft below sea-level), by two main companies—the Cyprus Mines Corporation of Skouriotissa and the Hellenic Mining Company. The principal areas of operation are in the Lefka area south of Morphou Bay, around Tamassus, 15 miles south west of Nicosia, at Limni, near Polis and at Kalavasos, roughly midway between Limassol and Larnaca. Ores are exported from the specialised ports of Xeros and Vasilikos.

The rise in world prices for basic materials also stimulated other branches of the Cyprus mining industry. The asbestos mines, for instance, formerly worked by the ancient Greeks and Romans who made the long-fibred variety into cremation sheets, were reopened at Amiandos, in the heart of the Troodos mountains, in 1907. Operated by the Tunnel Portland Cement Company of Great Britain, production has been increasing steadily since the 1930s and, with the greatest reserves of this mineral in the Middle East, Cyprus is second only to Spain in the world export tables.

The benefits from the asbestos quarries do not, however, go unquestioned. For one thing, the quarry workers are liable to suffer from pneumoconiosis, caused by the permanent lodgement of asbestos fibres in the lungs. Water is polluted, and soil erosion accelerated. But although these effects can be minimised by careful controls, the despoilation of the landscape cannot be hidden. For the mines consist of a number of open quarry benches of varying heights tumbling down the steep mountainside. Whereas this might be thought to add 'industrial drama' to a somewhat monotonously afforested mountain landscape, it remains true that many acres of forest, adjacent to a proposed national park, have been destroyed for ever.

Copper pyrites and asbestos form the main items of mineral exports and provide the greater part of the employment for the 5,000 workers in the mining industry. But mines are also worked for chromite (in the Troodos area near Mount Olympus; the ore is transported by aerial ropeway down to Kakopetria for treatment) and for umber (at Troulli in the district of Larnaca, exported raw and powdered). Many other minerals, too, are found in the island, but not in commercially exploitable quantities. As Constantius wrote in 1819:

> And gold, the end and aim and active cause of all man's efforts and energy—gold, which the corruption which [*sic*] daily swells and spreads among us tends to fix as the necessary and inevitable curse upon which our warmest and most earnest wishes are set—this too has veins in the land.

There are, additionally, extensive quarries for limestone and gypsum, mainly from the St Hilarion deposits in the Kyrenia range. Among other stones locally worked is the Cyprus Marble:

Page 125 (above) Moni electric generating station near Limassol, oil fired and with a full capacity up to 180,000 kilowatts; (below) The port of Famagusta, the biggest in Cyprus, dealing with the bulk of exports and imports

Page 126 (left) A typical village café, open virtually round the clock; *(below)* Flute-player in the yard of a village house

this is not of great economic importance, yet because of its durability and exquisite warm golden colour when polished it is widely used as a flooring material in richer village houses.

Mining leases have been granted for oil exploration since before World War I, and drilling continues in the Mesaoria and in an area east of Limassol. It has, however, not yet been discovered in any worthwhile quantities.

The salt lakes

Salt is extracted near Larnaca from the largest of the four lakes, covering altogether 1·3 square miles. In winter, these lakes fill with sea-water by underground seepage to a depth of 6 to 8ft; in spring the seepage stops, for reasons not yet convincingly explained. The water evaporates, and a crust of salt, a few inches thick, then remains on the surface. Local people have their own, less scientific but more attractive explanation of the source of salt in the water. After Lazarus had been brought back to life by Christ, he came to Cyprus, landing near Larnaca. To quench his thirst, he asked a peasant woman living near the town for a few grapes. She refused, and Lazarus showed his anger by transforming her vineyard into a salt lake.

Apart from three centuries of neglect of the lakes during the period of Turkish rule, salt has been collected at least since the times of Pliny; in Venetian times it even became an important export. The method of collection today is identical to that described as in use in the sixteenth century. Between fifty and sixty labourers walk on to the dry surface of the lake along narrow paths; they carefully scrape the salt from the surface and load it into pannier bags. These are then carried to the shore by long caravans of mules. The salt is piled into small mounds, then collected and shaped by hand into two pyramidal structures, where it is left for twelve months as part of the process of purification. The lake, which supplies all the needs of the island—about 3,500 tons each year—is a government monopoly: it is, indeed, a punishable offence for private

H

citizens to collect their own salt, either from the lake or from the sea-shore.

WATER

The availability of water is always a cause for concern in the island, and not just because droughts limit household supplies in most summers. The principal source of water has been, and still is to a decreasing extent, the underground aquifers. Two-thirds of the town drinking water, for instance, comes from boreholes. Throughout the main agricultural areas of the island, and particularly around Famagusta, the small wind pumps needed for mechanical irrigation are a major feature in the landscape. However, although a licence is required for the installation of each pump, the aquifers are gradually becoming overpumped, resulting in this source either completely drying up, or else in sea-water seeping into the water-table. The consequent salinity of the supply in a number of areas is adversely affecting the crops, and goes to explain the parched brown leaves of many thousands of otherwise healthy citrus trees inland from the Famagusta coast. New salt-resistant strains of orange trees are being developed, but the future for irrigated crops in this part of the island does not appear bright.

Nor does the answer lie in the utilisation of perennial springs, for there are few in the island, and these can only be utilised locally. One of the more abundant of the springs is at Kythrea, near Nicosia, which has an average flow of over 5 million gallons of water per day, and at one time supported thirty-five flour mills. Despite refutations by geologists, local people believe that this water derives from the mountains of southern Anatolia, some fifty miles distant, coming through a geological fault under the sea-bed. The basis of this widely held belief is a tale that a shepherd in Turkey one day dropped his silver goblet into a stream and that, soon afterwards, an identical goblet was washed out in the spring at Kythrea.

The island is therefore dependent on maximising the use of

surface water resources. Since there are no perennial rivers—
though river-beds are much in evidence in all parts of the island
to cope with spate flows in winter—there is a substantial
reliance on dams, mainly in the foothills of the Troodos massif.
The programme of dam construction was initiated between
1899 and 1901 by the British administration, and many
petitions were soon received for new dams in all areas. This
initial programme was not a great success, however, and was
discontinued until 1940. Many of the early dams are now
silted up and crops are grown on their surface; others bred
malaria mosquitoes. It was, however, not until recent years
that the problem of the shortage of water has received any
systematic study. But despite the efforts of the government's
Department of Water Development to speed and co-ordinate
the construction of dams, the supply of water is still lagging
behind demand, and desalination seems the only long-term
solution.

AGRICULTURE

Cyprus, known once as *Makaria* ('Blessed') on account of the
exceptional fertility of its soils, is still predominantly an agricultural country, with farm produce comprising over half of the
island's exports, and the sector employing 40 per cent of the
total labour force. Yet, despite its importance and its impressive
growth of output over the last decade or two, it is grappling
with many problems of tradition. Farm holdings, for instance,
are nearly all small—the average size is under 15 acres, whereas
the minimum adequate size for a dry-land farming unit is 30
acres—and they are scattered, with the 70,000 holdings divided
into some 660,000 individual parcels.

This pattern results directly from the system of inheritance
whereby a man is legally obliged to leave his property, to be
divided in equal portions, to all his surviving sons. That the
holdings are small and fragmented both hampers the spread
of mechanisation and obliges farmers to travel very many miles

between fields in the course of a day's work. The one advantage, often quoted as a reason for the continuation of this system, is that the fragmentation of holdings minimises the risk of damage to crops from localised storms. This is, however, insufficient economic justification and, in an attempt to raise the level of productivity, the Ministry of Agriculture is pursuing a policy of land consolidation. This elementary measure of land reform entails the voluntary pooling of a village's land and consequent redistribution on more rational lines.

The pattern of tenure is further complicated by the fact that water rights, which can be so limited as to be measured in minutes per fortnight, may be held independently of the ownership of the land itself. In addition, the trees on the land may be in yet another holding. Together with the fact that most fields are unenclosed and unfenced, this can lead to many bitter arguments among the farming community.

Even though most farms are owner-operated, nearly half of all landholders do not regard farming as their principal occupation; and even more will have second jobs either in their villages (as, for instance, coffee shop proprietors) or, more often, in the towns. It is also not unusual to see families travelling out from the urban areas to work their fields on Sundays, either by car or in the family bus. The increasing influence of the towns is, in Cyprus as elsewhere, causing many men to abandon farming completely; but the total numbers working on the land stay constant at a little under 100,000 as increasing numbers of women take over their husbands' agricultural tasks when the latter move to urban occupations.

Agricultural yields are thus very low in comparison to the potential of the land but, under the guidance of the Ministry of Agriculture, are steadily improving. Oxen and donkey may be seen together pulling wooden ploughs as in biblical times; but the number of tractors has increased from a mere 39 in 1939 to 4,300 in 1965. Corn is still threshed in some areas with a flint-studded board pulled by bullocks; but here again the old threshing boards are more readily found in museums. The most significant technological advance has been in the expansion of the area of irrigated land. Government investment had set the pace in this field, although much has also been achieved through private initiative. The importance of irrigation should not be underestimated: some 10 per cent of cultivated land is permanently irrigated, but this accounts for almost 50 per cent of the total agricultural production.

Other activities of the ministry include the determination of the dates between which the various crops may be harvested and the establishment of minimum prices at which they may be sold. Research into development of farming methods is conducted at the government's Agricultural Research Institute, at its main station of Athalassa, near Nicosia, and at Morphou, Paphos and Saittas. Its brief is to solve current agricultural problems, to evaluate scientific advances in the light of local conditions and to determine how the agricultural potentialities of Cyprus may be developed most fully.

Cyprus, too, has a most advanced system of agricultural co-operative organisations, dating back to 1909. The necessity for their introduction was summed up in 1878 by R. H. Lang, the acting British consul:

> The horse-leech which bleeds the peasant is the usurer from whom he borrows to pay his taxes and subsist until his crop is matured. These advances he procures at almost fabulous cost. Not only does he borrow at an interest of 2 and sometimes 3% per month, but the lender insists on being paid in kind, which results [in being credited for lower quantities than actually delivered and at lower prices than usual] ... The cost of advance exeeds 40% per annum.

The modern co-operative movement now has branches in all the larger villages, and handles the marketing of some 90 per cent of all agricultural produce. And despite continuing complaints from the private sector, it has also expanded its area of activities. Not only does it run a banking service which, having

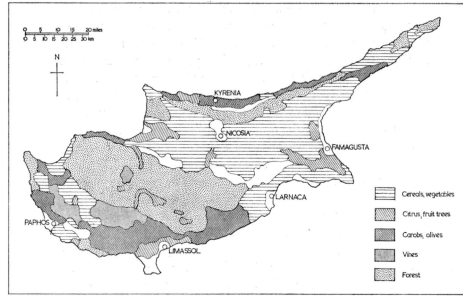

AGRICULTURAL LAND USE

the advantage of being exempted from taxation, is in direct competition with the commercial banks, but it has also branched out into fringe activities such as cinema management.

Agricultural produce

Of all the many crops grown in Cyprus, the vine, although covering less than 10 per cent of the total cultivated area, is said to support directly or indirectly the livelihood of half the families on the island. The development of viticulture can be traced back to antiquity: the biblical reference to the vineyards of Engadi are thought, for instance, to relate to a plantation near Paphos; the original vines for the Champagne and Madeira grapes may have come from Cyprus; and the knights commander of the Crusades initiated the production of the sweet wine, now known as commanderia, in their vineyards near Limassol.

132

There are now over one hundred varieties of grape grown in the island, mainly on the chalk plateaux in the Troodos foothills. Over 3 million gallons of wine are produced each year, of a good quality light red and white, the exports going principally to the English market. Sherry is also produced, again for England since very little is consumed locally. Zivania, a spirit of 50° proof made from the distillation of the remnants after pressing for wine, is exported to eastern Europe as a base spirit. The remaining production is of table grapes and sultanas, together accounting for only 5 per cent of the total grape harvest.

The backbone of the agricultural industry is dry-crop farming, mainly of cereals in the plains and the chalk plateaux, occupying around one-third of all agricultural land. Cyprus may, indeed, have been one of the original homes of wheat: certainly bread ovens and grindstones, very similar to those in use today, have been found in neolithic sites throughout the island. Cyprus now meets all its own requirements of barley and needs to import only a small proportion of its total wheat requirements. As cereals are such an important part of the national economy, the effect of weather on production can have quite dramatic repercussions. Variations in the climate can cause greater fluctuations in output than for most other crops, although hardship to the producers is minimised by government subsidy in times of drought.

It is the fruit trees, however, and particularly citrus, which account for most of the agricultural exports. Cyprus oranges are acknowledged to be of a very high quality, both the Jaffa-type grown at Famagusta and Morphou and the Valencia variety from the Phassouri plantations near Limassol. Yet citrus production in the island embraces not just these table oranges but sweet and bitter oranges, grapefruit, tangerines and sweet and bitter lemons as well. Other fruits are produced in relatively small quantities, but sufficient for the home market and, in some seasons, allowing a small surplus for export. They include peaches, apricots, bananas, dates, nuts, figs and

133

pomegranates, not forgetting the olive, in addition to most of the fruits which can be grown in cooler climates.

Industrial crops are gradually becoming of less importance, although small areas of cotton are still cultivated. Sugar-cane was grown until the seventeenth century, and the sugar storage barn can still be seen at the crusader castle at Kolossi. Flax, sesame and aniseed are other crops that, grown only in small areas, have almost disappeared from Cypriot fields. Yellow-leaf tobacco, too, is grown in the Karpas—practically all for export, since it does not appeal to Cypriot taste.

The sector which is receiving the greatest attention because of its export potential is market gardening. This is, however, not a new development: Heyman and van Egmont noted in 1759 that, in Famagusta, there 'are no suburbs but the houses lie about half a mile from the town, in the open country, with every one its garden, which here makes a very luxurious appearance'. All types of vegetable are cultivated, from those now common in northern Europe—the cauliflower was first grown in Cyprus, near Kythrea—to the more exotic produce: asparagus, okra, artichoke and squash. Yet modern methods of production are slow in reaching the island, and the yield per acre is consequently often less than half that attained in other countries. Tomatoes, for instance, have traditionally been grown along the ground, thus being marketed bruised and ripened on one side only; it is proving difficult to gain acceptance for the idea that they should be grown up posts.

Of the livestock in the island, the pig has survived its virtual extinction during the Turkish period when it was banned by Moslem religious laws; its numbers, in fact, increased threefold between 1963 and 1970. Goats and the fat-tailed sheep are widespread in the lowland areas only, since they are prohibited from grazing in most of the mountain districts; easily confirmed is the Cypriot saying that 'a sheep likes the dry plain even if it eats earth'. As important as their meat and skins is the milk which is converted into cheese in every village. Up-to-date dairies of Friesian cows are multiplying near the towns; and Cyprus has become self-sufficient in eggs, poultry and pork. Taken as a whole, animal husbandry provided about 35 per cent of gross agricultural production in 1970.

Fishing

Fishing is of little importance in the economy since the coastal waters around the island are deficient in the plankton necessary for the survival of fish. Apart from sea bream and the small but tasty red mullet, there are few edible varieties in the inshore waters. To develop the industry, therefore, the Department of Fisheries encourages trawl fishing, mainly in the Nile Delta, by means of loans and subsidies. The department also carries out biological and oceanographic research to exploit local stocks.

An attempt was made in the fifties to stock the reservoirs with carp; but this experiment was a complete failure, since the fish was rejected by the market as being associated in people's minds as the food given to hospital patients by the British authorities. The experiment has again been revived, but this time using trout. Although initially received with some scepticism, it seems likely that trout will eventually form an acceptable part of the Cypriot diet.

MANUFACTURING INDUSTRY

Cyprus first became an industrial nation during the Ptolomaic period, in the 250 years before Christ, with the development of shipbuilding, weaving and metal working. The later opening up to the West of the Middle East by the Crusades, however, changed the economic base from manufacturing to trading. The prosperity of the Middle Ages was followed by centuries of neglect and oppressive taxation, first under the Lusignans and later under the Turks so that, by the time of the British occupation, the island's economy was almost exclusively based on

agriculture. Although the colonial government effected substantial and much-needed improvements to the administrative
machinery and to the communications infrastructure, only a
few small firms became established in the island before the
1950s. The climate of confidence fostered by the new government after 1960 to some extent counteracted the unsettling
influences of the struggle for independence; but the manufacturing sector remains small and underdeveloped: it employs
less than 15 per cent of the total workforce (around 35,000
people in 1970) and contributes an even smaller proportion to
the national income.

Production is largely destined for the domestic market; over
half of the total output is of food, drink and tobacco. Textiles,
clothing and furniture-making are also relatively substantial
sectors, with minerals and metal products taking only a small
share although experiencing a fast rate of growth. This industrial structure implies a proliferation of small firms—the average
establishment employs only three people—and relatively low
productivity. Apart from the limited size of the local market,
one of the reasons for the relative lack of progress is the determined preference of the Cypriots for imported goods. The
government is continually making efforts to counteract this
tendency with 'Buy Cyprus' campaigns.

Since the government places an emphasis on the eventual
establishment of manufacturing industry as the mainstay of the
whole economy, it is selectively encouraging the development
of industry, within the context of a market economy. This has
involved, for example, government participation in certain
undertakings such as the oil refinery complex at Larnaca,
planned to process up to 750,000 tons of crude oil annually, and
sufficient to meet local needs at least into the late seventies.
The refinery will, it is hoped, also stimulate the growth of
secondary chemical industries. The government's tariff policy,
too, is used to give, in the words of the Second Five-Year Plan,
'some degree of protection in cases where the industry has

prospects of developing into a viable industry both from the point of view of quality and price'. Tax-free holidays are given for the first three years of operation of a new enterprise in addition to investment allowances. Manpower training is undertaken for industry by the government's Productivity Centre, established in 1963 with financial and technical assistance from UNESCO.

Perhaps most important in the special circumstances of Cyprus is the creation of industrial estates in the main towns. Hitherto, factories were scattered haphazardly in the commercial centres and in the residential areas of the towns; and, as land prices rose prohibitively, new units became established on the main roads leading out of the towns. This pattern has brought with it the usual economic and environmental problems of unco-ordinated growth. Most of the urban areas are now zoned against industrial use, and government-sponsored estates have been set up which offer land to industrialists on reasonable leasehold terms.

Traditional crafts

Any comparison of items exhibited in the archaeological and folk-art museums with the wares displayed in contemporary town bazaars gives sufficient proof that the hand-made goods on sale today for use around the home are directly related to those which were made in ancient times. Thus coppersmiths still produce the same utensils as did their forefathers centuries earlier. The simple yet beautiful forms produced by contemporary potters are, in many cases, identical to those found in Bronze Age tombs. Jewellers work the most intricate designs in gold and silver, but with a standard repertoire limited to the same basic patterns as when the church was their sole customer. There is no question but that the standard of workmanship of the Cypriot is unexcelled; but tradition is supreme, meaning that the only changes in style are directly due to changing techniques of production.

One of the principal exports of traditional craft work is of the lace made in the villages of Kato and Pano Lefkara. These twin settlements (*Kato* means Lower, and *Pano* Higher) nestle in the folds of the chalk hills in the south east of the Troodos range. Set among thinly scattered olive trees—which, by virtue of their oil, provide the only alternative employment for the villagers other than lace manufacture—it is difficult to distinguish the white-rendered houses and the surrounding countryside from a distance. Here, the old patterns of lace have been handed down from generation to generation since the time when the craft was first taught by their Venetian masters. Every visitor to the villages today is regaled with tales of the admiration shown for the cut and drawn thread-work and the white embroidery, *asproploumia*, by Leonardo da Vinci; and the visitor is shown designs identical to that which for centuries has adorned the altar in the cathedral of Milan.

In the same way that lace is associated with the two villages of Lefkara, so most other craft industries of the island are highly localised. This is due in many cases to the existence nearby of the materials needed for the specialised work, but in certain instances the reasons for a particular location are lost in the mists of history. Baskets of split reeds and willow twigs are made, for example, principally at Livadhia (near Larnaca) and at Mesoyi (Paphos): both villages are near supplies of reeds; and both met local needs, in the one case baskets for export of grapes, and in the other for the general needs of the port of Paphos; but demand has now long outgrown local reed supplies. Or again: the village of Moutoullas in the Troodos mountains is the only place where the wooden troughs for dough are made; once in the middle of a thickly afforested area, it now has to import timber from other parts of the island. And only at Kornos can be found the naturally occurring mixture for producing the red pottery that is characteristic of the district.

With the progress of mechanisation, many of the craft

138

industries are disappearing: there were 6,000 weavers in the island at the beginning of the century; 4,500 in 1946 and only 600 in 1960. One of the implications of this decline is that hand-made goods peculiar to the island are fast becoming collectors' items; and the Cypriot is well aware of the potential value of many things in his house or farmyard that, a few years earlier, he would have regarded as rubbish. A case in point is the dowry chests, *sandouki*, traditionally given to each daughter on marriage to hold her dowry linen. Although these are still made in a few villages, and in Akanthou in particular, most are now destined for export. Usually made of local pine or walnut, the front of the chest is shallowly carved with stylised designs of birds, cypress trees, palaces or churches and, often, the double-headed Byzantine eagle. The carving of these chests, themselves small works of art, is a continuation of the tradition of carving the iconostases of churches. Despite the fact that few made nowadays remain in the island, it would be an artistic loss for Cyprus if the skill of making the chests were to disappear.

TOURISM

Tourism, a mixed blessing that tends to overtake poor but beautiful countries, escalated rapidly in Cyprus in the sixties. The island has, indeed, all the prerequisites for a successful holiday centre: abundant sunshine, clean sandy beaches, a multitude of interesting antiquities and, above all, a friendly and hospitable local population. If it were not for the political crises that recur periodically, the number of visitors would no doubt be even greater. As it is, tourist arrivals increased twenty-fold between 1960 and 1970, to make tourism the third largest 'industry', after agriculture and the manufacturing sector. In 1969 the island drew over 125,000 long-term tourists, over one-third of them from Britain, attracted particularly by a common language and the fact that Cyprus is in the sterling area. A large but unknown number of recorded 'tourists' are, however,

CYPRUS

Cypriots returning home from England to visit their families;
and others are English families visiting their relations in the
British bases. But the residual number of 'unattached' tourists
is, nevertheless, considerable.

With the realisation of the economic benefits of tourism—
around £8·5 million (US $20 million) was spent in the island
by tourists in 1969—the government is making strenuous efforts
through the Cyprus Tourist Organisation and Cyprus Airways
to attract an even greater number of tourists. The government
participates in most of the international trade fairs and always
has a section on its stands devoted to the tourist trade. Tourist
offices are being opened in a number of northern European
towns, for it is from here and from Middle East countries that
the greater part of the increased trade is expected to come. One
of the major promotional aspects is that Cyprus, even in these
days of transcontinental travel, stands at the crossroads between
Europe and Asia, and between eastern Europe and Africa, and
is thus an ideal place for an international conference centre.

To date, the tourist boom has been accommodated in an
entirely ad hoc manner, with land being developed in individual
sites for hotels as and when it became available. And few
facilities other than hotels or residential flats have been provided. The results of this uncontrolled and unco-ordinated
development can be seen at their most destructive in Famagusta:
here, the hotels have been built so densely and so close to the
sea that most of the beach, once one of the loveliest in the island,
lies in their shadow for the greater part of the afternoon.

With this abuse of the environment, limited as it is, has come
the realisation that Famagusta can never become another
Miami Beach, and that Cyprus cannot hope to compete with
Majorca or Beirut on their own terms. The lesson has now been
learned and, although new hotel development proceeds apace,
stimulated by loans at favourable rates of interest, town-
planning controls are being introduced to prevent a repetition
of the Famagusta type of development elsewhere in the island.

Alongside this environmental control has come a move to improve other facilities for tourists, both local and foreign. A Hotel and Catering Institute is ensuring, for one thing, that standards of service meet the demands of the most discriminating visitors. The road network is being extended into parts where it will bring few direct economic benefits but yet open up areas of particular natural beauty. Private developers, for their part, are planning a number of yachting marinas around the coast; and the possibilities of a quiet, secluded holiday are being promoted abroad as actively as the night-clubs and discothèques were previously advanced as the main attractions of a holiday in Cyprus.

7   ISLAND COMMUNICATIONS

WALKING, although necessary at times, has never been the favoured method of movement in the island, perhaps a result of the debilitating heat and unhospitable terrain. Camels and horses are still seen around the island, but they are used more as a tourist attraction in the one case and as an opportunity for betting in the other. It is the donkey or mule that has always provided the most acceptable means of transport and is now only slowly being abandoned in favour of motor transport.

Indeed, until the arrival in the island of the car, goods and people were moved between towns and villages by an organised group of muleteers, themselves probably descended from Venetian settlers. Travel by this means was, by all accounts, reliable even though uncomfortable and slow—the journey of little over twenty miles between Nicosia and Larnaca, then the main port, took two days with an overnight stop in the *khan* at Athienou. With movement so difficult, there can have been little contact between people in different parts of the island: an English visitor to the island in 1845 wrote that, to the inhabitants of one village, even the '12-hours-away market of Nicosia . . . is for them the centre of the universe'. Until recently most Cypriots lived and died without ever having seen the sea.

The difficulty of the terrain, however, has proved no hindrance to the growth of car ownership: in 1924 there were around 400 cars in the island; this number had risen to 1,500 by 1938; to 16,000 in 1957; and to some 53,000 in 1971 out of a total of 83,000 vehicles registered. This means that one car is registered

Page 143 (*above*) The Cyprus moufflon; (*below*) The snow-clad Troodos massif, which covers most of south-western Cyprus and where skiing is popular. Olympus is the highest peak (6,400ft)

Page 144 (above) Cypriot girls in national costume dancing in front of Bellapais abbey, the most beautiful of medieval monuments in Cyprus; *(below)* Carnival procession, the high point of the annual celebrations in Limassol

for every four families; the rate of ownership in Nicosia is almost as high as it is in London, and statistics show that, in 1970, one out of every three people eligible to drive held a full or provisional driving licence. It is also one of the economic mysteries of Cyprus how such a high proportion of the population can afford to own and run the large luxury cars that constitute a large percentage of imports (the level of tax and insurance is of the same order as in the United Kingdom).

For the non car-owning household, there is a multitude of bus services linking the villages with the towns, although their timing is designed principally to carry villagers to and from the urban markets and their workplaces; going into the towns in the mornings, returning to the country in the late afternoons. Indeed, many of the owner-drivers of the 'village buses' combine their task with another, full-time job in the towns, driving both themselves and their passengers to and from work. These buses are by no stretch of the imagination comfortable and will no doubt eventually be replaced by more up-to-date coaches, but they are yet an integral part of the contemporary Cypriot scene. For they double their role as being carriers of people and goods: passengers must share the limited space with chickens, goats, cylinders of gas and furniture and indeed anything and everything that needs transporting between town and village.

The urban bus services do use more modern vehicles, but their services are erratic as well as being sparse or non-existent in the evenings and at weekends. Even at peak hours, drivers often prefer to fill their buses before starting a journey, ignoring the official schedules. Competition with the buses is increasingly being provided by taxis, both in the towns and in the larger villages. It is on the inter-town services, however, that the taxis really come into their own, operating at half-hourly intervals, with a door-to-door service if requested, and working with fares only marginally higher than those of the buses.

THE ROAD NETWORK

In ancient times, roads had been constructed only as a matter of necessity: a Roman map shows a sort of ring road around the island, linking the main towns; a Venetian map of Cyprus shows two bridges, but no roads at all. Even the few long-distance tracks remaining in Ottoman times were given no maintenance. The Turks did, however, attempt to build a road from Larnaca to Nicosia with locally conscripted labour and financed by a special tax; but the money was misused, and only a short length of the road was ever completed.

In response to local petitions, the British initiated a substantial programme of road construction, which has been continued with vigour since independence. The first stretch to be completed was a military road leading from Troodos to Limassol, followed soon by others linking Nicosia with Morphou, Kyrenia, Larnaca and Famagusta. Between 1892 and 1932 a law was in effect under which any village that wanted a road could have one: half of the cost was provided by the government, and every able-bodied villager was obliged to provide up to six days' labour on its construction.

By the end of 1969 the road network consisted of over two thousand miles of asphalted roads, administered by the government's Public Works Department and the municipalities, and a further two and a half thousand miles with a good gravel surface, under the authority of the Department of Forestry and the District Administration. This makes it now possible to motor to most parts of the island in relative comfort. With the exception of the roads linking the main towns, however, travel can be somewhat hazardous: most of the minor roads are only of one lane—9ft wide—albeit with hard shoulders; the edges are generally unprotected; and the roads, in following the contours, can take a very winding course. The gravelled forestry roads (over 750 miles in total length, and built mainly during

146

the British occupation) are particularly impressive, opening up the forests for development at the same time as providing access for tourism. The diversity and unpredictability of some of the roads provide ideal conditions for the Cyprus International Rally. This annual event, organised by the Cyprus Automobile Association and involving a 24-hour drive through the island's mountains, is rated amongst the most testing of all rallies.

The growth of car ownership has brought with it the usual environmental problems—flourishing petrol stations and unsightly roadside signs, fumes and noise. The problem is, however, most acute in the town centres which were designed, not as in most of Europe for horse-drawn traffic, but for pedestrians only. The municipalities have proved reluctant, with their limited financial resources, to supply any off-street car parking or, indeed, to compromise in any way between the needs of car users and pedestrians. The result is that the whole of the narrow road space in the main shopping and business districts is given over to the movement or parking of vehicles, leaving no room for people on foot; pavements are, in fact, the exception rather than the rule. To the initial displeasure of shopkeepers, however, a very few streets, in Nicosia and Limassol, have been provided for pedestrian-only use at certain times of day, resulting in a return to the more leisured and agreeable pleasure of walking down the main thoroughfares.

THE RAILWAY SYSTEM

The arrival of the first car in Cyprus coincided with the opening of the island's only public railway. Built initially to link Famagusta port with Nicosia, the first 37 miles of the narrow gauge (2ft 6in), single-track line was opened to traffic on 21 October 1905. Just over two years later, the line was extended for a further 24 miles to serve Morphou and, in June 1915 again to Evrykhou. This latter section of 15 miles in the Troodos foothills was designed to carry chrome as well as firewood to the copper mine at Skouriotissa; its opening was delayed by World War I, and the first train did not run until 1922.

The enthusiasm generated among the people of Cyprus by the new railway was such that requests for other lines were received from all parts of the island. A French firm was persuaded to suggest that it could build a railway to serve Larnaca; and the inhabitants of that town went so far as to petition Winston Churchill, when visiting Cyprus in 1907, for their own link to Nicosia. The benefits of the railway were not limited, however, to its users, since the water from the steam-engines, dropping on to the tracks, caused rich growths of grass which then attracted and fed herds of sheep, goats, cattle and even the occasional camel. But the public mania for railway development soon wore thin since, with a maximum permitted operating speed of 24 miles per hour, the one line by no means gave an express service. The story is still told of the engine driver, on his way to Famagusta, offering a lift to one of his friends walking in the same direction. 'No thank you,' was the reply, 'I'm in a hurry.'

The arrival of the motorbus in the mid-1920s served to hasten the decline in the number of passengers. The operating company tried to attract traffic by introducing passenger and freight road-feeder services but, in June 1932, the section west of Nicosia was finally closed to passenger traffic. More economies were made, among them being the construction of light petrol railcars at Famagusta in the thirties, with engines taken from farm tractors. These did enable higher speeds to be reached and, on the three trains each day, journey time over the 37 miles was reduced to as little as one and three-quarter hours. Steam was reintroduced in World War II, accompanied by an increase in the number of passengers. The situation was such, however, that camels had to be used for marshalling wagons in the Nicosia sidings.

Passenger traffic again declined after the war, and the railway came increasingly to depend for its revenue on the one-way freight traffic, predominantly exports of oranges. By 1950 it was clear that, if the service were to continue, much of the equipment would need to be replaced or modernised: the service had been losing an average of £6,000 (US $14,700) each year over the forty years of its existence. The modernisation scheme would cost around £400,000 (US $980,000). This money was not available, and the railway finally closed on 1 January 1952.

Some reminders of the railway can still be seen around the island, including Locomotive No 1 which was used both to build the line and to demolish it, rediscovered in 1953 and now preserved outside the police station in Famagusta. Many of the old stations and halts have been converted into coffee shops; and the line of the track east of Nicosia has been turned into a fast road to Famagusta. The avenue of eucalyptus trees on part of this section, first planted to protect the rolling stock from the sun, makes a fine memorial to the passing of the Cyprus railway.

EXTERNAL COMMUNICATIONS

For the greater part of its history, Cyprus has maintained close contact with the outside world, first through its export of minerals and timber, and later as a commercial centre at the time when Famagusta was the principal trading outpost of the Western world in the Levant. During the period of Ottoman rule, though, the ports were allowed to silt up and the opening of the new trade routes around southern Africa hastened the decline of Cyprus as a trading power. Even the Suez Canal benefited the island little: in the 1930s, exports were still being transported by caïque from numerous little coves and landing places near to the places of production.

Ports

The last few decades have seen an increasing realisation of

the need for good ports and harbours to stimulate trade. The island has good sea communications with Greece, less frequent scheduled services connecting with various ports in the Middle East, and no direct passenger service to England. Car ferries link Cyprus with a number of Mediterranean ports in Europe, Asia and Africa, and there are cargo services between the island and Europe, North America and the Middle East, on ships of at least nine different national lines. The Cypriot merchant fleet, too, created by the provision of special tax incentives, had, in 1970, a gross tonnage of about 1·5 million in almost 3,000 vessels.

Famagusta was the first port to be developed to meet modern requirements, contemporaneously with the construction of the railway. This is the port closest to Nicosia and hence to the main consumer market and distribution centre. It is also traditionally associated with the export of citrus fruit, both from the local groves and from the large plantations around Morphou. The outer harbour was completed by a Polish technical assistance mission in 1965, and is able to take large vessels of a berth not exceeding 7·5–10 metres. Container ships call at Famagusta, and the port's facilities were extended in 1971 to meet this trade.

The island's other main port is at Limassol which, too, was being enlarged to give an artificial harbour with 800 metres of quayside. This is designed to be the main passenger port, although liners will continue to dock at Famagusta as well. It also handles the considerable volume of exports from the town and region, particularly of wine and other grape products, and carobs.

Political pressures have been at least as important as strict economic rationale in the development of the island's ports since, in addition to the facilities at Famagusta and Limassol, there are numerous other minor harbours offering both general and specialised handling facilities; there is considerable doubt about whether they are all justified in this island of little more than half a million people. The largest of the secondary ports is at Larnaca, and there are discussions about reviving Paphos as a fourth international trading centre. Additionally, oil is discharged at Dhekelia, Vassiliko, Limni, Xeros and Karavostassi.

Air transport
Widened business contacts and the commercial horizons being opened up by the possibility of exporting fruit, vegetables and flowers to northern Europe by air have both helped to make the Cypriots more conscious of air travel. But it is the tourist trade that has contributed to the bulk of the 12 per cent per annum increase in traffic at Nicosia's International Airport during the 1960s. For Cyprus is only a few minutes' flying time from Beirut and, in the early seventies, around four hours from London. Scheduled air services connect Cyprus with the neighbouring countries of the Middle East, with centres in western and eastern Europe, East Africa and, most importantly, with Athens and London. The island is served by sixteen international airlines, the largest of which is Cyprus Airways, carrying almost one-third of all airline passengers travelling to the island.

Apart from the military airfields in the British Sovereign Base Areas, the only airport is the Nicosia International, with a runway of 8,000ft and large modern terminal buildings.

THE MASS MEDIA

When the British first arrived in Cyprus, the island did not possess a single printing press. The lack was, however, soon corrected, and the first newspaper—a bilingual weekly, printed in Larnaca—was published in 1878. It was not until April 1920 that a daily paper was published, but that ceased publication after nine days. Today, with illiteracy virtually eradicated and with political activity so important in the life of the island, newspaper publishing is a flourishing business. There are at least eight daily papers in Greek and Turkish, free from censorship and representing all shades of opinion. The only foreign language newspaper is the English *Cyprus Mail*, published seven days a week: although its typography is occasionally errant, it has a wide coverage of local and international news.

The broadcasting services, too, are extensive for such a small population which, in 1970, owned 21,000 television sets and 136,000 radios. The principal service is given, under government charter, by the Cyprus Broadcasting Corporation (CBC): it has two radio channels, one broadcasting for eighteen hours a day in Greek, including a wide variety of educational programmes for elementary schools, the other carrying news and entertainment programmes in Turkish, Armenian and English, with a programme of classical music for a few hours each day. The CBC television station, transmitting from Troodos and Kantara, can be received in all parts of the island. It is financed partly by licences (evasion of payment is rife) and partly by advertisements. The greater part of its output is necessarily imported, from Greece, Britain and America, but 30 per cent is produced locally—programmes of a high quality, mainly news, documentaries and plays. Since 1967, the television service has also been carrying regular programmes for secondary schools. CBC also plays an important part in the island's artistic life: it has a theatre and film club, supports a symphony orchestra and publishes a number of books whose titles range from *Philosophical Anthropology* to *Learn Greek*.

The British Forces Broadcasting Service (BFBS), although aimed primarily at the large service audience, also has a wide following among Cypriots, particularly for its programmes of popular music and sport. Radio Bayrak ('The Voice of the Turkish Cypriot Fighters') broadcasts mainly in Turkish, but also puts out music programmes and news in Greek and English.

Telephone and telegraphic services in the island are provided by the public Cyprus Telecommunications Authority (CYTA).

Subscriber trunk dialling is in operation between the principal towns, and the usage of telephones is widespread even where distances are so short and face-to-face contact relatively important. By the end of 1969, there were 495 villages connected to the telephone network, and over 28,000 private subscribers, giving an average of 1 telephone for 22 people. The services of CYTA are supplemented in the remoter areas of the island by telephones provided through the Department of Forestry.

8   TOWNS AND VILLAGES

FOUR millennia of foreign domination have left surprisingly little mark on the Cypriot way of life. The physical remains of ancient civilisations, it is true, can be found in each corner of the island, almost in every field. But the conquerors remained generally aloof from the local people, content merely to exact taxes and retain in the island a base for trading. The language, the customs, the building forms, the life styles of the Greek majority have stayed basically unaltered over the centuries. And, although the increasing influences of Western culture are slowly starting to effect changes, the traditional way of life is still reflected in the settlement pattern, in the design of the villages, in the architecture of the country.

The lack of fish in the seas around the island means that the people of Cyprus have always looked towards the land for their livelihood. This, together with well-founded fears of pirate raids in the Middle Ages, has resulted in the only coastal settlements being the main trading ports—Limassol, Larnaca, Famagusta, Paphos and Kyrenia. Yet alone of the towns, only Nicosia is inland. Each of them has widely differing functions, its own individual character and completely different historical backgrounds; yet they share much in common.

The archetypal Cypriot town is centred on the old core which, in the case of Nicosia and Famagusta, is bounded by the original Venetian fortifications. The old town, with its narrow and congested streets, still contains many of the facilities central to the town's functions: shops and bazaars, warehouses and bus depots, offices and administrative buildings. Outside

154

the centre, however, the town has been growing at a rapid rate, radially outwards; and secondary centres have developed which take away much of the commercial business from the core. Each town, too, except Kyrenia, is now divided between Greek and Turkish sectors, separated by the local equivalent of Nicosia's Green Line. And in every town, too, there is a sharp contrast between the prosperity of the Greek quarter and the relative poverty and lack of development of the other.

Nicosia was chosen by the Lusignans as administrative capital for defensive reasons; and has grown accordingly. Limassol, Famagusta and Larnaca all owe their importance to their possession of tolerably good harbour facilities: Limassol is growing as a manufacturing town and a service centre for the nearby British Sovereign Base Area of Akrotiri, whereas Famagusta has become the island's principal tourist resort. Larnaca, on the other hand, lost out on the growth rate in the sixties, although it is slowly re-establishing itself with a new industrial base. And, in complete contrast to the other towns, Paphos and Kyrenia have the character of overgrown villages: the first little more than a marketing centre for the poor villages of the immediate district; and the second almost exclusively a tourist and commuter centre.

Although the prosperity and economic growth of the island are initiated in the towns, over half of the population still lives in the villages. Statistics may show that the island is relatively sparsely populated—it has 170 people per square mile in comparison with 830 people per square mile in England and Wales—but it is difficult to travel for more than one Cypriot mile (an obsolete measure of the distance that can be travelled at a stretch by a laden donkey) without coming across some small settlement. Of the 585 villages in 1970, over half had a population of under 500.

In very general terms, villages are located only in areas where there is both a supply of fresh water and soils suitable for cultivation. Rivers, being dry for most of the year, do not attract settlements; deep valleys, too, are avoided because of their tendency to attract frost in the winter. More often than not, the sunny side of a slope is preferred.

Roman and medieval maps show that isolated homesteads were once much more common than today; now, in fact, all settlements are of the compact type. The scarcity of water supplies has caused families to draw together to a common source. The inherent sociability of the Cypriots, too, has been a major factor in determining this pattern. More importantly, though, reasons of security have in the past demanded that people should live in close groupings. It is, however, more difficult to generalise about the form that the villages take: they vary from the extremely densely built up villages of the Mesaoria, typified by Lefkoniko—narrow streets, no gardens or other open space except for the central square—to the widely scattered villages which have perennial irrigation, like Lapithos with its extensive groves of lemon trees surrounding almost every house, or Rizokarpaso at the end of the Karpas peninsula, with houses widely separated to give private land adjacent to every dwelling. As for other features, Christodolou points out that many villages are built to include some observation post, from which approaching visitors can be seen well in advance of their arrival. Otherwise, the only feature that Cypriot settlements have in common is the village square, the centre of everyday life, surrounded by the coffee shops, themselves the main meeting places, together with the church, the school and other public buildings.

URBANISATION

Cyprus, in common with all countries throughout the world, whatever their stage of development, is experiencing a continuing movement of the population from the country to the towns. But unlike the situation in most other countries, this process of urbanisation in Cyprus has brought with it few attendant problems and disadvantages. The scale of the movement is moderately large: in 1931, for instance, about 22 per cent of the population lived in the six main towns; by 1969 this proportion had risen to 39 per cent, with an even higher number living in the villages immediately outside the metropolitan boundaries. Put another way, the urban population had risen by 250 per cent over the 38-year period; during the same time, the rural population had increased by less than 40 per cent.

Yet this level of increase is one that has been accommodated without severe physical disturbances: the supplies of public services have expanded adequately to meet the increased demand, and the environmental consequences, although not in keeping with the character of the rest of the island, are relatively well ordered. It is remarkable, too, how the growth in urban employment has kept in step with the growth of the urban population—although the essentially bazaar-type economy means that a considerable number of jobs can be created from a very small economic base. And the high level of land prices prevailing at the end of the sixties meant that increasingly few people could afford to buy or rent dwellings in the main urban areas.

The islanders have a strong respect for property and personal rights and so, even after the intercommunal fighting of the mid-sixties, were not tempted to develop squatter settlements or in any other way occupy land to which they had no legal rights. The movement of people is thus turning from the main urban and suburban areas into the surrounding villages, where land prices are lower and from where it is easy to commute to work into the employment centres. Thus between 1946 and 1960 the population of Nicosia was increasing at a rate of over 4 per cent per annum; between 1960 and 1969 this had fallen to little over 2 per cent per annum. Yet during this latter period, the villages within fifteen minutes' drive of the town were growing at around double the urban rate.

There is, indeed, a very high level of commuting to work in Cyprus, perhaps not so surprising since most of the population lives within an hour's drive of one of the six towns. (It is probable that about half the total workforce of Nicosia commutes to work from outside the town boundaries.) The pattern is evidenced further by the annual summer migration of workers of all socio-economic groups from Nicosia to the Troodos mountains where they will rent an apartment and each day drive down to work in the plains. That commuting is such an advanced phenomenon is also partially explained by the excellent network of roads throughout the island, supplemented by an extensive public transport service. Apart from the financial advantages of commuting over permanent migration to the towns, it has the added attraction of allowing people to live in their own villages with their families, and thereby retain their former security as well as small agricultural holdings with which they can supplement their incomes from employment in the towns.

If, then, people are not moving to the towns in the same numbers as previously, they are nevertheless adopting urban behaviour patterns. The accessibility of the towns, the spread of literacy and broadcasting (most villages have a television set, at least in the coffee shop) and the general diffusion of urban culture through recent migrants back to their families still in the country, are all increasing urban-type aspirations. The influence of the towns is thus spreading outwards: the old customs that have survived for so many centuries are now in the process of disappearing; suburban-style buildings, symbolic of the wealth and education of the inhabitants, are being erected in all villages.

This is not to say that there are no longer differences between urban and rural ways of life; of course there are. For one thing, urban cash incomes are approximately double those in the rural areas, although the latter have been increased partly through extensions of the market by specialised trade agreements, partly through the extension of credit to rural producers, and partly as a result of the military bases which have given a considerable amount of employment to villagers. But it is the towns that have been growing in importance, above all dominated by Nicosia which itself provides nearly half of the urban employment. The greater part of all shopping is now undertaken by villagers in the towns; these, too, are the centres of entertainment. Education is being centralised so that, even though elementary schools are to be found in most villages, it is to the towns that pupils will increasingly be coming for secondary and higher education.

The corollary of this is that life in the villages is getting even slower, with so many facilities being drained away to the towns. And since the rural-urban migration is predominantly of younger and more active members of the community, the future for the villages is not promising.

ARCHITECTURE

Apart from churches, mosques and monasteries, there are few buildings in use today that are more than a hundred years old. In part this is due to the impermanency of the materials used for construction, often no more than mud and straw in the plains; and in part because the stone used in the otherwise more durable buildings has always proved useful in other, later, construction works. The pattern of plundering stones from Greek and Roman buildings in Salamis in order to build the Venetian Famagusta, the same stones being later used in the construction of the Suez Canal, has been repeated time and time again, if on a less dramatic scale. Even from the relatively recent period of the Turkish occupation, few buildings remain apart from the *khans*, the travellers' inns, in the walled city of Nicosia.

The rural domestic architectural styles have, however, stayed virtually unchanged since post-neolithic times: strong similarities have been noticed between the contemporary Cypriot dwelling and ancient Greek houses. The traditional structures are almost entirely functional but, as with so many things that have developed organically in response to need, are no less attractive on that count. They are built according to the maxim, 'A house as little as can accommodate you, and land as much as you can see'; they are designed for people who lead their lives in the open air, people who have asked for little more than shelter for themselves and for their animals.

In the countryside, the materials used have customarily been taken from local sources, thus blending in perfectly with the landscape. In the lowland areas, these are usually sun-dried mud bricks—made of a mixture of earth and straw—which are durable when well maintained with plaster, but subject to rapid decay when left without regular maintenance. Today, many deserted villages made of these mud bricks can be seen literally dissolving away into the original dust. With the exception of a small handful of villages which are built out of red clay bricks or out of wood, stone is used elsewhere, either exclusively on its own, or in combination with mud. In the Troodos area, for instance, the igneous rocks are broken into large blocks for building purposes; and in other places, limestone and sandstone are the predominant materials.

Although differences can be found relating mainly to variations in the agricultural customs of different districts, the construction of the house follows a more or less consistent pattern. The floor is either of earth or, in the more prosperous houses, of slabs of the local golden marble. The ceiling, supported by arches of timber or stone, is generally of earth resting on reeds or wattle, this in turn being supported on cross-beams. The roof itself is flat in the lowland areas, so that it can be used for drying agricultural produce and for sleeping out during the hot summer months. The house consists of three rooms: one used for most domestic purposes including eating and sleeping, one for storage and the other for animals. Characteristically, the house will be built around a courtyard, which is used extensively in the same way as an indoor space. Arranged around the yard, and probably under a grapevine arbour, will be the well, the beehive-shaped clay oven and the outdoor lavatory, shaped also something like the oven, but larger.

This traditional type of housing is being replaced throughout the island by suburban styles of dwelling construction, the change being contemporaneous with an increase in wealth. In physical terms, this produces an incoherent environment of monotonous dissimilarity in the towns; in the villages, the new building styles are, quite simply, incongruous. Favoured is the one- or two-storey single family dwelling, liberally decorated with pastel washes, standing a regulation distance of 10ft away from its neighbours.

The whole often has an unfinished air, largely because many individually owned building plots (again of standard, regulation size) are left undeveloped until such time as the daughter of the owner is old enough to marry and in need of her own house. It also results from the fact that many houses are designed so as to allow extra rooms to be added when the family grows larger. These additions to the structure may be made either on top of the existing house, by the side or, in a good number of cases, actually underneath the dwelling. In this latter case, the second storey is completed first but with the ground floor left empty except for the necessary supporting pillars.

High-rise buildings are becoming increasingly common in the centres of the larger towns. They are architecturally no more distinguished than elsewhere in the world.

Town planning

The practice of town planning in the island has been in a constant state of flux since the mid-1940s when the British colonial administration invited the distinguished town planner, Sir Patrick Abercrombie, to prepare a statement on the island's needs. From that time, the Department of Town Planning and Housing has been responsible for administration of the few houses built by the public sector and for handling the development control machinery of the Streets and Buildings Regulations. Until late 1972, however, there was no comprehensive town planning law, although a number of draft bills had been rejected by the House of Representatives.

This does not mean that there is no need for town planning or that the responsible department is inactive. The speed of urbanisation, the growth of motor traffic, the increasing impact of tourist development, all call for some form of co-ordination and control, inimical though this may be to the Cypriot nature. The government is well aware of these needs and is attempting, through its existing powers which include zoning restrictions against particular types of development, height restrictions and others, to meet the environmental requirements of a country which, through its rapid economic development, is coming to realise some of the less attractive consequences of growth.

HOUSING

The upward trend of building, together with the opulent villas that line the approach roads to the towns, give a first impression of generally good housing conditions. Noting also the absence of squatter settlements (with the exception of a very few gypsy encampments) and of slum areas in general, as well as the holiday homes being put up in the more attractively situated mountain and coastal districts, conditions could be said to compare very favourably with those in many other countries. Such a superficial approach, however, conceals some of the considerable difficulties that individual families must face in order to get a roof over their heads.

The root of the problem is the dowry system which, although widely accepted as leading to hardship, is none the less tolerated as part of the traditional way of life in the island. A young husband will generally have a house provided for him by this means; but if he becomes the father of two or more daughters, he must start making considerable financial sacrifices. It is admittedly a great achievement for a father to build four or five houses out of an apparent annual income of around £500 (US $1,225), and it is not uncommon. The mechanics of financing are relatively straightforward: all the members of the family will contribute towards payment for the house, as part of their duty; and those with time and some constructional ability will assist in the actual process of building. Problems are slightly mitigated if the father's house was designed to take extensions, for then the daughter and her family may live in their own dwelling under the same roof as her father, and there is thus no necessity to purchase more land. In certain towns with a large foreign population, and especially Limassol, it is always possible, even though being strictly illegal, to rent the house to a foreign family at an inflated rent and for the Cypriot family to move to the one or two outhouses at the bottom of the garden, and live there in sadly unhygienic conditions.

Land prices are high and continually rising—many instances have been quoted of rises exceeding 100 per cent per annum—and since construction methods are not of the greatest efficiency, the total cost of a house and land in the late sixties averaged some twelve times annual family incomes in the towns, and only slightly less in the villages. And yet a high rate of construction of new dwellings has been achieved against all the odds—reaching over 3,500 new dwellings each year in the early seventies—and almost exclusively built through private initiative. The government has built only a handful of subsidised houses, which are sold to the occupants on a rent-purchase scheme; and though the municipalities have built rather more, judging by the number of 'Associations for the Homeless', these are still insufficient to meet the demands of those in the lowest income groups. The Turkish administration, for its part, has constructed a number of flats and houses for the refugees after the intercommunal fighting, but the size and standard of these does not match up to those found in the private sector.

House purchase is made difficult, too, through the lack of any building society or housing bank for the lending of money to prospective purchasers. They must therefore look either to their own resources or to the banks, which will generally lend money for periods not exceeding seven years and at rates of interest close to the legal ceiling of 9 per cent. In his own way the Cypriot manages to overcome these obstacles, and to build his own house, there being relatively few speculatively built estates. Surprisingly, too, the new houses are amongst the largest in the world, averaging almost six habitable rooms each.

Yet a walk through some of the remoter villages, or even along the back streets in the town centres or older suburbs, will show the poor conditions in which many people are still living. In 1960, the latest year in which there was a housing census, 23 per cent of the people were living at a density of four or more to one room; and only one in every five village houses had running water. Many families were using a shared earth closet; and damp was coming through the unplastered mud walls. Overall, housing conditions are certainly improving; but concurrently, the relative standards enjoyed by the poorest section of the community have been declining over the past few decades.

THE SIX TOWNS

Nicosia

Nicosia, one of the few island capitals that do not lie on the coast, has risen to its present importance as the administrative capital only since Lusignan times. The settlement was, so legend tells, founded by Lefcon, son of Ptolemy Soter, in 280 BC as *Ledra*—hence the name of the main shopping street today. It grew to some importance after being the market centre for a small but rich agricultural district in the thirteenth and fourteenth centuries. Although it was sacked by the Egyptian Mamelukes in 1426, the Venetians readopted Nicosia as their capital on arrival in Cyprus in 1489 and then, in 1570, erected considerable fortifications around the old city. The choice of

Nicosia as capital was on the grounds that the site could be easily defended, yet Alexander Drummond—British consul at Aleppo—commented in 1754 that 'its situation is extremely ill judged for a fortified town, there being several hills upon one side of it from whence the houses might easily be battered down'.

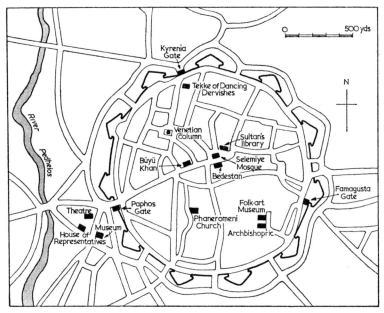

CENTRAL NICOSIA

These fortifications, designed to withstand the newly invented cannon, were strongly built of earth faced with stone that had been plundered from eighty churches along with monasteries, cemeteries and other buildings of town notables. The walls are circular, with eleven bastions which bear the resounding names of the Venetian officers in charge of their defence—Constanza, Quirini, D'Avila, and so on. All the buildings outside the walls were, at the same time, destroyed and razed so as to leave a clear line of fire from inside the city.

165

Much of the Venetian military works have escaped subsequent destruction and provide an impressive feature of the contemporary city. The moat has now been partially filled in and, although landscaped in parts, has in others succumbed to modern pressures in being used for car parking and commercial purposes. The original gates into the town, too, still stand—the Paphos Gate, Porta Domenico; the Famagusta Gate, Porta Guiliana; and the Kyrenia Gate, Porta del Proveditore, over which is the inscription, 'O Mohammed, give these tidings to the Faithful: Victory is from God and triumph is very near. O opener of doors, open for us the best of doors.' The irresistible increase in traffic has, however, caused new roads to be pushed through the walls and the whole city centre is now surrounded by an important ring road.

The true charm of Nicosia lies within the palm-lined walls. But even this is fast disappearing: the old houses with their wooden balconies overhanging the deep streets are being replaced by multi-storey blocks of flats; and peasants with their baskets of eggs mingle none too happily with heavy lorries delivering the latest goods to the shops.

Since the division of the town into strict Greek and Turkish quarters, the Greeks have taken over most of the city's trade, and it is in their sector that the city is at its most lively. The Turkish sector, being the poorer, is correspondingly the more dilapidated; but to the visitor it is certainly the more attractive of the two quarters, retaining as it does the characteristics of a Middle East town before the inrush of Western influences. Some considerable effort is being made by both the Greek and the Turkish authorities to preserve the ancient monuments that lie in this quarter, the mosques and churches, the palaces and the gardens.

The greatest gem is the former Latin cathedral of St Sophia, now the foremost place of Moslem worship in the island, the Selemiye mosque. The cathedral was consecrated in 1326, but never wholly completed. Although the Turks, on first occupying

166

the building in 1570, destroyed the furnishings and statues, they respected the overall architectural concept. Internally, it is now very simple, its dignity enhanced by the whitewashed walls; and the only jarring note is struck by the mihrab, a niche built into the south transept to indicate the direction of Mecca. From the outside, it dominates the whole town, with twin minarets complementing its Gothic harmony.

Around the Selemiye mosque lie a number of other buildings of great beauty and interest: on its south side stands the Bedestan, a fourteenth-century church, used as an Orthodox cathedral during the Venetian occupation, later converted into a market. On the assumption, probably false, that the church was named after Thomas à Becket during the Third Crusade, there was a proposal at the end of the last century that the building should be restored for Anglican worship. It was, however, taken over by the Evqaf (Moslem Religious Foundation) for use as a grain store. Today it stands empty.

In the same general area are the island's few remaining examples of Ottoman architecture: the Sultan's Library, now containing excellent specimens of Turkish and Persian calligraphy; the Tekke (Convent) of the Dancing Dervishes, now used as the Turkish Folk Museum; and the two *khans*, the Büyük Khan (Great Inn) and the Kourmardjilar Khan (Gamblers' Inn).

Outside the walls, the city is growing in wealth and importance, expanding haphazardly outwards and upwards, engulfing the old suburban villages with little recognisable form. Most of the 110,000 or so inhabitants live in this new part, the greater number of them in the southern, Greek, areas, sharing it with the main government offices, the Presidential Palace (occupying the building which, in colonial times, was Government House) and with the modern shopping district. The one building of historic and architectural interest that had been left by the Venetians outside the city walls, the palace of the Lusignan kings, was demolished by the modernising British in

167

1879. And few of the old yellow-stone villas survive even from the beginning of this century, having been built in locations which can now justify a much more modern type of development.

Nor does the city offer much attraction by virtue of its setting: the hills commented on by Drummond are now covered with suburban buildings, and viewpoints are few. From the outskirts, one is certainly aware of the Kyrenia and Troodos mountains rising to the north and west; but these are no more than a distant promise of relief from the heat and dust of the modern city. Even the river Pedheios which winds through the city from south to north holds few attractions, since it is generally waterless for the greater part of the year and, in any case, is largely inaccessible due to being surrounded by private land.

Nevertheless, by way of compensation for the lack of other natural beauties, successive inhabitants of Nicosia have systematically planted the few parks and many and extensive private gardens with a bewildering variety of flowering plants and shrubs. Whereas in a cooler climate one might find lawns, here, where water is a rare commodity, bougainvillaeas and poinsettias cover the ground. For most of the year Nicosia is a blaze of colour, which affords some compensation for its generally drab appearance.

Limassol

A good-natured rivalry exists between the people of Nicosia and those of Limassol, the second largest town in the island. Each claim their town to be the more prosperous, the more lively, the more beautiful. Despite the pre-eminence of Nicosia in commercial fields, it is difficult to dispute many of the claims of the Limassolians for, with a progressive and individualistic municipality, Limassol has grown into a town of some considerable importance.

The town has a short history: when Richard Coeur de Lion landed at Amathus, a few miles to the east of the present situation, Limassol did not exist. It rose to importance only in the Middle Ages with the growth of the island as a trading power. Indeed, the only building of real historic interest is the castle, built by the Turks soon after their occupation of Cyprus.

A number of new hotels have been constructed on the outskirts of the town in association with the development of the port for passenger traffic; but Limassol is not really a tourist centre. It does, however, serve a number of other functions in addition to being a port: as a market and administrative town for its district; and as an industrial centre, particularly for the processing of drinks—wines, spirits, beers and soft drinks—for this is the nearest main port to the grape-producing areas of the chalk plateaux. Its prosperity also derives from the servicemen and their families from the British Sovereign Base Area of Akrotiri, many of whom are quartered in the town itself.

Limassol contains two effective centres, both in the Greek sector. One is in the old town, congested and outdated perhaps, but still full of vitality and character. The streets generally radiate outwards from the sea-front promenade—open air cafés on the seaward side, hotels and offices on the other, a place for taking the airs and, during carnival time, a mass of rejoicing people. The other centre lies astride the main Nicosia–Paphos highway, built originally by the British as a military road, now referred to as 'the bypass' even though the town has spread way beyond its northern side. Here are the supermarkets and night-clubs, the chicken bars and car showrooms, the area most frequented by the families of the resident British servicemen. Beyond the bypass, the streets lead out to rows of near-identical villas in the north.

Yet the real character of the town springs from its continual liveliness. Possibly this is occasioned by the presence of the large wine and beer factories; and certainly it is helped by the two annual festivals. The wine festival, held in late September to mark the end of the harvest, is a great opportunity for celebrations, with alcohol flowing freely from public fountains. The other is Carnival which, although held islandwide at the start of Lent, has its main manifestation in Limassol, with people flocking to the town from all corners of Cyprus.

Famagusta

Famagusta—'Hidden in the Sand'—is a city of two completely separate quarters: the medieval walled city, exclusively occupied by Turkish Cypriots, and the Greek 'suburb' of Varosha. The rise to importance of the old city is not fully chronicled, although apparently originating from the activities of merchants based on Acre during the early Crusades. By the Lusignan era, the city had become famed for its wealth and extravagance; the Venetians fortified it; but many of the finest buildings of this period were destroyed in the battle with the Turks in 1571.

The old town is today largely in ruins and presents a near-deserted appearance: 365 churches once stood within its walls, and those now left serve as shelter for the poorest families and their livestock. Even in 1743 Richard Pococke wrote of the town that 'the present buildings do not take up above half the space within the walls, and a great part even of these are not inhabited'. Much of the town is still open terrain or wasteland, an ideal playground for the few children. And even the developed parts, apart from the small centre, contain few of the new villas that characterise the residential areas of the other towns, thereby being much more reminiscent of a village.

The central point of old Famagusta is the magnificent Latin cathedral of St Nicholas, consecrated in 1326. Thanks to its later conversion to use as the Lala Mustapha mosque, the building has not only remained standing where many minor churches have been allowed to fall into decay, but it has escaped many of the architectural modifications which have been made to contemporary European cathedrals. It thus remains as an outstanding example of original Gothic architecture. The square in which it stands, bounded on the opposite side by the palace of the Venetian Providitore, had once the reputation of being the largest in the Western world. Famagusta, too, is the 'seaport in Cyprus' of Shakespeare's *Othello*: there is little doubt that the governor of the city in 1508, Cristoforo Moro, is identifiable with Shakespeare's Moor. Due to this link, the citadel of old Famagusta, which bears the winged lion of Venice above its main entrance, is now known as 'Othello's Tower'.

The new town of Varosha presents a complete contrast: it contains all the buildings of commercial and administrative importance, the night-clubs and the luxury hotels. It is jointly to these hotels—fronting directly on to one of the best beaches of the island—and to the port that Famagusta owes its present prosperity. The port itself lies immediately under the Venetian defences of the old town. It is from here that most of the agricultural produce of the Mesaoria is exported, and into where the greater part of the island's imports are directed.

If, then, the tourist area and the sea-front could be in any Mediterranean coastal resort (albeit cleaner than many), and if the port could equally well be anywhere else in the world, the residential sectors of the town are perhaps unique. For here the orange groves on the rich and formerly well-watered soils of the outlying areas intermingle with the villas, not only providing most of the inhabitants with their own supply of fresh fruit, but also serving to perfume the whole town with the distinctive sweet scent of orange blossom.

Larnaca

From its former position as the island's principal city in Phoenician times, the main port of embarkation of pilgrims to the Holy Land and the centre for the diplomatic corps during the Ottoman period, Larnaca has declined, now being a small town of only 20,000 inhabitants, trying hard to find a place in the economic structure of twentieth-century Cyprus. The town is indeed chiefly famed for being the birthplace of the Stoic philosopher Zeno, and for having given a home to Lazarus, who became Bishop of Larnaca. The remains of the saint were stolen from the church that bears his name in AD 890 and taken to Marseilles; but a marble sarcophagus remains, with the inscription, 'Lazarus, the friend of Christ'.

Like other Cypriot towns, Larnaca presents a sharp contrast between the old and new quarters. The former has a somewhat old-fashioned, riviera, appearance, facing the water-front: the centre for the Sunday promenade. Amply provided with coffee shops and kebab stalls, this area comes into its own at the time of the sea festival of Cataclysmos. The new town is not very distinguished, and owes its air of relative well-being in large measure to the economic boost provided by the stationing there of British servicemen from the Dhekelia Sovereign Base Area.

Since Larnaca's position as an international port had been largely usurped by Famagusta and Limassol, and since the coastline, being rather bleak, was of no attraction to tourists, little new investment was made in the town in the fifties and sixties. It was government policy, however, that all regions and towns should share equally in the general growth rate, and certain measures were therefore taken in an attempt to revive the local economy. These included the construction of the oil refinery which, although giving little direct employment, was intended to stimulate secondary industries. One of the island's first industrial estates, too, was opened at Larnaca, albeit at an inconvenient two to three miles outside the town boundaries. This show of public confidence in the future of Larnaca stimulated a certain amount of private investment, including the construction of a yachting marina and a holiday centre.

Paphos

Some confusion has arisen over the number of places which are known as 'Paphos': the name is usually used to refer to the administrative capital of the Paphos district, also known as Ktima. This is an inland town, whereas the port of Nea (New) Paphos lies two miles to the south. Palea (Old) Paphos, now the village of Kouklia, is some ten miles east of Ktima, off the

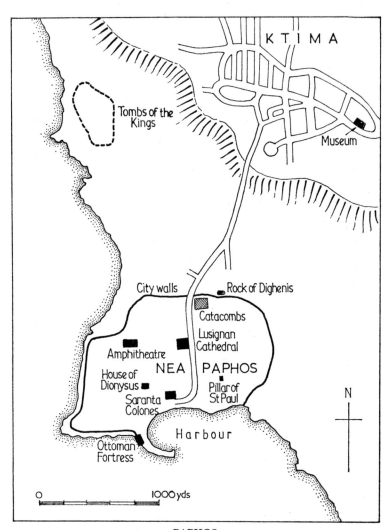

K T I M A

Tombs of the
Kings

Museum

City walls

Rock of Dighenis

Catacombs

Lusignan
Cathedral

Amphitheatre

NEA   PAPHOS

House of
Dionysus

Pillar of
St Paul

Saranta
Colones

N

Harbour

Ottoman
Fortress

0   1000 yds

PAPHOS

road to Limassol. The confusion may be further compounded by the discovery of yet another port east of the present harbour.

Nea Paphos, now with only a few thousand inhabitants, lies on a site formerly occupied in neolithic times and said to have been re-established later by Agapenor in 1180 BC. A conflicting theory, however, suggests that the 'modern' city was not founded until the end of the fourth century BC, by Nicocles, the last king of the Paphos kingdom. The city developed until it became the capital of the whole island under Roman occupation. The history of the present town of Ktima does not begin until the seventh to the tenth centuries AD, when raids by pirates forced the inhabitants of the port to move to a safer and, incidentally, healthier, site inland. Earthquakes and disease finally brought about complete abandonment of the old port, which was not re-established for human habitation until Ottoman times.

Even now, only a few hundred people actually live in Nea Paphos, many of these either making their living from fishing— a small and delightful harbour has been reintroduced here—or from catering for tourists, since the restaurants on the sea-front are reputed to serve the best fish in Cyprus. Yet the whole has a curiously abandoned air: apart from the cafés and an incongruous naval installation in the harbour, the area is dominated by grass-covered ruins, tens or thousands of years old. The few houses are set back towards Ktima, as if not wishing to intrude upon the history of the place.

The Paphos area contains a spectrum of all the most important periods of Cypriot history, starting from the temple of Aphrodite at Kouklia and with relics of the legendary Dighenis. The Bronze Age is represented by the Tombs of the Kings—rock-hewn burial places, though not in fact for royalty, that were later converted for Christian use. Nea Paphos has a large Hellenistic amphitheatre, and there too is the pillar to which the town's Roman governor had St Paul bound. Also in Nea Paphos are the remains of a few Roman buildings, one of which, known as the House of Dionysus, contains the famed Paphos mosaics. Catacombs and a number of well-preserved churches remain from the Byzantine period; but the great Lusignan cathedral is now completely in ruins, much of its stone having been used for the construction of later buildings. Similarly, the earlier harbour defences of Nea Paphos were replaced by an Ottoman fortress.

Being the town farthest from the island's capital and separated from the rest of Cyprus by the Troodos mountains, Paphos/ Ktima has remained somewhat isolated. Little industry has developed there apart from a wine factory, and the town is off the main tourist circuit. This has resulted in lack of 'progress' relative to the other towns: the retention of old customs, closer family ties, and less intrusion of contemporary affluence manifested by motor traffic, night-clubs, high buildings and the like. True, the public buildings at the entrance to the town, built in Italianate style, are more imposing than municipal buildings in other towns; but the remainder of Paphos keeps a flavour of the old Cyprus that has been lost to most of the eastern half of the island. The whole centre, indeed, has the air of a market-place: open-fronted shops selling few imported goods; narrow streets congested with donkeys; and the occasional palm tree growing incongruously in the middle of a courtyard. Even the new housing areas farther out, although poorer than in the other towns, have a spaciousness, giving the impression of a gentler speed of life, consistent with the hospitality for which Paphos is famed.

Kyrenia

Kyrenia is the most picturesque of all the Cypriot towns, the one best known to the English community and unjustly famed as the favoured place of retirement of ex-colonial administrators. The town was founded by Achaean colonists in the tenth century BC, later to become a full city state. But it was not of great importance in the overall political structure of the island until it was fortified by Byzantium. The castle, which dates from this time, was strengthened and enlarged by the succeeding Lusignan and Venetian rulers. It was used again as a place of imprisonment during the EOKA troubles of the 1950s, although even then prisoners succeeded in escaping by the simple expedient of climbing down on knotted sheets.

Despite having a history longer than any of the other five towns, Kyrenia is the only one that does not act as a market centre for the region, since its position as such is usurped by the neighbouring twin villages of Lapithos and Karavas, and by Nicosia which is only 15 miles distant on the direct road. It has, then, become first and foremost a holiday resort, centring on the little yachting and fishing harbour. Although accommodating only 5,000 inhabitants in 1970, it looks set for growth also as a commuter village to serve Nicosia.

9   FOR THE TOURIST

NUMEROUS and good guide-books are available for the visitor to the island (a selection of these is listed in the bibliography at the end of this book), and plentiful information on questions of interest to tourists is given willingly by the offices of the Cyprus Tourist Organisation and by Cypriot embassies in most European countries and in the United States. The present chapter, and indeed the book as a whole, is not intended to duplicate the information that can readily be obtained from these sources, but rather to abstract certain of the more basic items of knowledge necessary for the traveller and to add one or two hints that are not contained in other published works.

TRAVEL TO THE ISLAND

Cyprus is served by several daily direct flights from Heathrow Airport, London, by Cyprus Airways, BEA and BOAC, with a scheduled flying time of four to five hours. Most European capitals, too, are linked to Cyprus by air, with flights at least once each week. In addition, a number of flights are directed there from centres in the Middle East and Africa. Travel to the island by sea is, however, a much more rewarding, if more difficult, matter. Except on cruise ships, there are no regular passenger sailings from northern Europe, although berths can sometimes be obtained on cargo ships at short notice. There are, however, regular sailings from a number of Mediterranean and Black Sea ports on ships which also carry cars at relatively high rates.

L

The average, English-speaking, reader of this book is unlikely to require a visa to enter the island, or to be troubled by
currency restrictions. Cyprus is in the sterling area, and the
value of the Cyprus pound is tied to that of the pound sterling.
(The pound is subdivided into 1,000 mils, although shopkeepers continue to refer to shillings—equal to 50 mils, or one
twentieth of a pound—and to piastres—equal to 5 mils.)
Vaccination certificates are not normally required although,
when there is any doubt over these matters, advice should
always be sought from official tourist offices.

English is widely spoken by Greeks and Turks, certainly by
most hotel- and shopkeepers and by businessmen; some
difficulties of communication may be encountered in the villages,
but the schoolmaster or priest is usually able to help. Other
European languages are spoken to a lesser extent though, with
an increasing number of tourists from northern Europe,
German and French are becoming used more widely.

The greater number of tourists arrive in the height of summer,
in July and August; there are lesser peaks around Easter and
Christmas caused by expatriate Cypriots returning home on
holiday. Midsummer should be avoided when possible, for the
island is more crowded then (even if never to the extent found
in most other recognised Mediterranean resorts), and it can be
unpleasantly hot. If the purpose of the visit is primarily relaxa-
tion, the late summer months of September and October are
ideal: the air has then lost some of its extreme dry heat, whilst
remaining in the 80s Fahrenheit; and the sea is perfect for
swimming, averaging 77° F even in October. March, April and
May are, in many ways, the most delightful months: the sun
shines for over two-thirds of all daylight hours, but has not yet
burnt away the spring blossoms of flowers. Sunbathing and
exploration are both possible at this time of year. The winter
months, on the other hand, can seem very cold at times,
particularly when the wind blows off the snow-covered Troodos
mountains. But, for the visitor interested in exploration of the

antiquities or of contemporary Cyprus, even if there are a few rainy days, there is the compensation that many prices are lower in winter-time.

Cyprus offers a choice of over 140 hotels with a total accommodation capacity of some 10,000 beds, ranging in price and comfort from the Cyprus Hilton and other de-luxe class hotels in the main towns, down to the smallest hotels, barely frequented by foreign tourists, in the mountain and coastal villages. The greater number of the better class hotels are in Nicosia, Famagusta and Kyrenia; and it is to the two seaside towns that most package holidays are directed. Prices are generally reasonable, and compare very well with those prevailing in most of Europe.

All hotels are classified by the Cyprus Tourist Organisation. Those in the higher categories offer every modern standard of service and amenity; but care should be taken when visiting hotels in the (lowest) fourth class which, although clean, afford somewhat spartan conditions. The latter, however, provide a very good way of getting to know the island and the islanders for those tourists who prefer not to be shut off in one of the luxury beach hotels from all but their fellow holidaymakers.

Apart from the hotels, there are around 10,000 beds in other forms of accommodation, ranging from apartments for rent to beds in private homes. It is possible to sleep overnight in most monasteries without charge, although a monetary offering is expected of visitors. There are, too, a number of youth hostels in the island; and, although camping is officially discouraged, there are several places where it is perfectly possible to camp provided that all the usual basic rules are observed. A number of private camp sites have been established at certain points around the coast; these are not well advertised, and it would be well worth the time of prospective campers to enquire of the

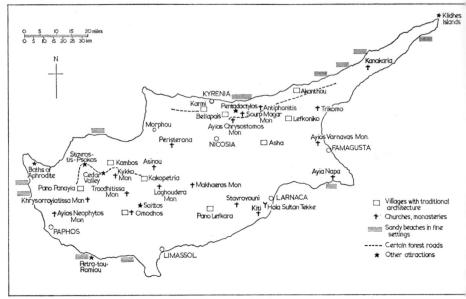

TOURIST ATTRACTIONS

foreigners resident in Cyprus where these can be found. Full details of accommodation available can, of course, be obtained from the Cyprus Tourist Organisation.

WHERE TO GO

Too many people who visit Cyprus never leave their hotels in Kyrenia or Famagusta other than to go to the beach. They thereby miss much of the best of the island, since this is largely to be found outside the main towns. Travel by bus is not recommended, unless on one of the many organised excursions, for timetables, where these are observed, are generally geared to the needs of commuters only. Taxis offer the best way of moving between towns: they are cheap and offer a reliable door-to-door service.

Otherwise, there are a good number of car hire firms on the

island. Most makes of car can be hired at reasonable rates; petrol is cheap, driving is on the left, as in England; and a visitor's driving permit can be obtained from the licensing office on production of an English driving licence. The driving habits of the Cypriots may cause some initial alarm to the uninitiated, but although the Highway Code may not always be observed, the principal rules of driving are soon understood; then, motoring in this uncrowded island becomes a real pleasure.

Within such a small compass, Cyprus offers a wealth of different experiences, and there must be few people who could not enjoy a stay in the island to the fullest extent. Whatever the main field of interest, it would be wrong to spend any length of time in the island without sitting for at least a few hours in one of the small coffee shops; for it is here that the visitor will be able to meet the Cypriot at leisure, and in a comparatively short time learn more about contemporary life than he could in many weeks of sightseeing. It should be remembered in this context that the Cypriot will normally expect to act host even in casual encounters, and that it is considered impolite to leave a meeting before the coffee cups have got cold.

Historic sites

For those whose interest lies in gaining an understanding of the history and art of the island, there follows a short list of the more important sites and buildings outside the main towns. They are selected for their interest to visitors who are not well versed in archaeology, history or architecture. Comprehensive individual guide-books to most of these places can be obtained either at the site entrance (there is usually a modest entrance fee) or from the Cyprus Museum in Nicosia.

> *The Castles* of the Kyrenia range are all spectacular: possibly St Hilarion, a few miles north of Kyrenia town, offers the finest views; certainly it is the best preserved and calls for less physical effort in exploring it than the other two, Kantara and Buffavento.

Monasteries and churches abound: the most famous of all is Kykko monastery, 20 miles west of the Troodos centre. Ayios Neophytos, near Paphos, the home of the first neophyte, is cut into a rock face. The frescoes in the churches of Asinou (20 miles south of Morphou) and Antiphonitis monastery (on the eastern part of the Kyrenia range), are world famous; as are the mosaics in the charming church at Kiti, west of Larnaca.

Khirokitia, midway between Nicosia and Limassol, is the best preserved and most interesting of the neolithic sites.

Salamis, 4 miles north of Famagusta, can occupy visitors for several days with its Hellenistic, Roman and early Christian ruins.

Curium, 10 miles west of Limassol, is the island's other principal Roman site, with a reconstructed amphitheatre, baths, stadium and the Sanctuary of Apollo.

Aphendrika is a Byzantine town on the north coast of the Karpas peninsula and, although remote and difficult of access, has a good number of beautiful ruined churches.

Kolossi Castle, 15 miles west of Limassol, dates from Crusader times; apart from the fort itself, the domed sugar store is of interest.

Bellapais Abbey, above Kyrenia town, is an essential part of every tourist itinerary.

Hala Sultan Tekke, west of the Larnaca Salt Lakes, themselves justifying an excursion, is an important—and picturesque —Moslem shrine and mosque.

Vouni, set on a conical hill 10 miles west of Morphou, is a magnificently sited palace of the Persian period; but the access road, narrow, unguarded and with numerous sharp bends, should not be attempted by nervous drivers.

Beaches

The island offers plenty of scope for underwater swimming and diving, since the water is particularly clear and, apart from

the attractions of exotic fish and other creatures living underwater, many parts of the coastline still have extensive areas
covered with fragments of ancient pottery. It is unlikely that
anything of great archaeological value or historic interest will
be found in the closest waters (although the wreck of the oldest
known Greek ship was found off Kyrenia by a fisherman in the
mid-1960s); but this should not deter the amateur from
searching for his own Greek or Roman amphora. It should be
noted, however, that export from the island of any antiquities
is strictly prohibited unless a licence has first been issued by
the Cyprus Museum.

By contemporary standards, the beaches are barely polluted
by oil, and the sandy beaches are among the finest in the
Mediterranean. Nor are they particularly crowded, even in
the peak season, although it is usually necessary to drive for at
least half an hour from the main coastal towns to find a completely unoccupied beach. The best swimming is to be found
on the north and east coasts, the least crowded and most
extensive beaches on the relatively remote Karpas peninsula.

The villages

There are few villages in the island completely without
charm; yet so many in the more accessible areas are being
developed in a characterless mid-Mediterranean style. There
follows a short list of certain of the villages off the beaten track,
but connected to the main routes by asphalted roads, that have
retained worthwhile groupings of traditional Cypriot dwellings.

Karmi and Bellapais, on the northern slopes of the Kyrenia
range: the first is largely untouched by tourist development,
perhaps because it lies in the shade of the mountains for
much of the year; the second, made famous by Lawrence
Durrell, has been 'tidied up', and so makes a more direct
appeal to Western eyes. Both offer superb views.

Akanthou, farther east but also on the Kyrenia range, and

Pano Panayia, 20 miles north west of Paphos, have very fine groupings of traditional Cypriot domestic architecture, displaying the Byzantine arches and vine-covered courtyards to their best advantage.

Kakopetria, bypassed by the main road from Nicosia to Troodos, is one of the best examples of the wood-built mountain villages.

Politiko, 12 miles south of Nicosia, and *Tokhni* (midway between Nicosia and Limassol, and just off the direct route), or a dozen and one other villages in the Troodos foothills, have great charm in their stone-built houses.

Kythrea, 8 miles north east of Nicosia, falls into no such easy classification: much of its interest derives from the stream running down through the village, feeding the many water mills, turning the kebab spits and acting as the focal point for all village life.

Walks and drives

Cyprus is not an island for any but the dedicated hiker, since the metamorphosed rocks in the more attractive areas can be very hard on the feet. Yet a number of extremely pleasant walks can be found, particularly in the mountain areas. The track running along the top of the ridge of the Kyrenia range, with its numerous side ways, can give an endless variety of views. And it is an exhilarating experience to travel, either on foot or on one of the individually organised donkey rides, along the path between Bellapais and Buffavento castle; a good day should be allowed for this route. A further rewarding excursion, giving at the same time an opportunity for examination of some of the more interesting of the island's flora, is around the Acamas peninsula. Anyone intending to visit this area should, however, first make enquiries about the permitted days, since it is used by the British Army as a training and firing area.

Many of the unsurfaced forestry roads give unsurpassed views for drivers and their passengers with strong nerves. Although it

184

would be difficult to single out any particular routes, the long day's drive from Kykko monastery, passing Cedar Valley, through the forestry station of Stavros-tis-Psokas down through the village of Pano Panayia to Paphos, will give a taste of the best of Cypriot mountain scenery as well as permitting an excursion to the moufflon game reserve.

The Cyprus Government publishes a range of good maps of the island, ranging from the 6in to 1 mile motoring map and a tourist map of the Troodos region which shows roads, footpaths and places of interest, to the more detailed maps for specialist use.

WHAT TO EAT

When eventually the visitor has become familiar with the foods of the island, then he can be said to know Cyprus itself. For as the Cypriots are not a particularly gastronomic people and their everyday diet is rather simple, they do not force their food on to foreigners. On the contrary, in most hotels and restaurants in places visited by tourists, only European types of food are available. The principal deterrent to the enquiring traveller, however, is not the local food—which is wholesome and tasty—but the conditions in which it is served: always clean, certainly, but the décor of the local *maïrka* tends to appear a little scruffy and designed only for the local clientèle.

Cypriot cooking has strong family links with Greek cuisine which, in turn, is in many instances derived from the Turkish. The main ingredient of any meal (or so it may seem to the European) is olive oil, with liberal additions of herbs. Yet for the average villager, cooked meals are the exception rather than the rule: dark bread, olives and yoghourt, sometimes enriched with the addition of cheese, tomatoes and cucumber, forms the basis of his daily meals. Meat is eaten on Sundays, holidays and days of feasting—and there are numerous opportunities for the latter. On particular occasions the usual kebab or *klephtiko* will be complemented with smaller delicacies such

185

as *kupepia* (marrow leaves with a savoury meat filling) or *dolmas* (vine leaves stuffed with minced meat and rice). Most fish are grilled or fried—the most common and perhaps the tastiest is *barbouni*, red mullet—but squid and octopus are cooked in an enterprising variety of ways, and are usually surprisingly tender.

The *meze* is used for entertaining, and is the best introduction to Cypriot cooking; this is a meal or snack consisting of anything and everything that is to hand in the kitchen. When served in *maïrka* as an accompaniment to a glass of beer or brandy, one is offered a plate of groundnuts, a few pieces of a local white cheese (one, *halloumi*, is made from goat's milk matured with sage) and a few pieces of raw carrot or artichoke. At a different scale comes the *meze* which is a full meal of twenty or thirty dishes—and the uninitiated should beware of mistaking the first few for the whole meal—usually including *moussaka* (minced meat with aubergine in a bechamel sauce), *stifatho* (a rich beef casserole), roast and fried meats, vegetables, dips of *homus* and *tahina* and, always, olives, thick and creamy yoghourt and the flat *pitta* bread.

Cyprus, being one of those fortunate countries where fresh fruit can accompany every meal, has in consequence relatively few cooked sweet dishes. Cakes—which are rarely eaten as a part of the main meal—follow the standard Greek-Turkish recipes, generally made of almonds, honey and strips of *filo* pastry. Exceptions to this rule are generally cakes specific to a certain occasion, and distributed then only to relations and friends. A further speciality of the island is the *glykys*—literally, sweets. These are semi-crystallised delicacies, fruits, slices of peel or flowers. Each family has its own particular favourite which will be served to visitors with pride, to be eaten with a special silver fork.

Of all the drinks, coffee is drunk at any time and in any place. It is at the same time a refreshment, a means of passing the time and an expression of hospitality. The coffee is the Turkish variety, said to be ideally as sweet as sin, as hot as hell and as dark as night. It can also give a sight into the future, since cognoscenti can make predictions from the sediment left after drinking.

Wine is drunk at all times of day, even for breakfast. Favoured by tradition is the sweet and heavy wine of the commanderia type, although lighter wines more to the European taste are readily available. The latter are not subtle, although soft and full-bodied; they are best drunk with the local Mediterranean foods. Other alcoholic drinks have their particular seasons. Brandy, for instance, is regarded as a winter drink, a customary accompaniment to the Sunday feast, when up to a bottle per person may be consumed (with the price of a bottle equivalent to two or three packets of cigarettes, this is not a great extravagance). Ouzo, or raki, an aniseed drink taken with water, is popular in the springtime. In the hotter months, lager-type beer is drunk—at a rate of 25 pints per head of population each year.

10   POSTSCRIPT

OVER the past twenty years or more, Cyprus has been
continually in the headlines of the world's newspapers
as being a country of violence and discontent. True,
it has received its full share of domestic troubles, starting with
the nationalist uprising in favour of *enosis* and thus against the
occupying British forces; next between the Greek and the Turkish Cypriots attempting to work out a constitution that would
at the same time give a democratic form of government and
safeguard the rights of the minority; and later, with disagreement among various factions of Greek Cypriots as to whether
or not independence was the ideal status for the island. These
troubles have certainly caused considerable disruption to the
life of the country but, in the long run, may prove of less significance than the longer term and more deep-rooted developments
and changes in the island's society, economy and environment.

One of the major ill-effects that are said to have been caused
by the disturbances of recent years is that the economy, and
hence the standard of living of every Cypriot, has suffered. Yet,
although output fell in 1964 when there was widespread fighting
in the island, the economy has continued to grow at a rate which
would have been the envy of many other countries. The number of tourists, a good indicator of confidence in the economy,
has risen in Cyprus at around the same rate as in Yugoslavia
and Greece. And despite the internal turmoil, foreign companies have continued to make substantial investments in the
agricultural, manufacturing and tourist sectors. It is true,
however, that the Turkish Cypriots were unable to participate

188

fully in the economic boom of the late sixties, because employed predominantly in agricultural work and because they were, in any case, isolated by Greek sanctions from the mainstream of the economy. In practice, their isolation has only been made possible by occasional substantial grants from the Turkish Government in Ankara.

Foreigners visiting the island may be a little disturbed by the lack of willingness of Cypriots to discuss the political situation in public places because of fear. Yet, apart from temporary pressures by a small handful of extremist groups, Cyprus is as much a democracy as most countries of western Europe: political parties are free to voice their opposition to the line of the government; presidential and parliamentary elections, and those for the Turkish Cypriot Communal Chamber, are held at more or less statutory intervals; and the press, too, is generally unfettered by censorship.

The continuing social division of the island is more a matter for concern; and it is true that the longer Greeks and Turks remain without real contact, the more difficult the readjustment will be when a political settlement is reached. Children and soldiers of each community are being trained to regard the 'other side' as enemies, to be feared and hated. Already a number of children will have passed through their formative years without having experienced what life is like in a united island. It will be particularly difficult for them to adjust to a different life, where Greek and Turk are treated as equal.

It is improbable that the differences between the two will ever completely disappear, since religious beliefs will always prevent any substantial intermarriage. It is therefore unlikely, too, that the Turkish community will ever stop being regarded as a minority whose rights must be safeguarded by some legal or constitutional means. But the Greek Cypriots have always shown themselves to be adaptable to new circumstances; and the fact that Greeks and Turks have lived together in Cyprus for 350 years with no real racial disagreement until recent years, gives ground for hope that they will be able to do so again in the future.

It is likely to be more subtle changes that in the long run will alter the course of the island's history more radically than dramatic political events. One of the less easily perceptible changes is in the nature of society in which, for so long classless, class divisions are now beginning to emerge. The town dweller, for instance, is generally regarded as 'superior' to the villager, the graduate to the manual worker, the self-employed person to the civil servant. In part, these distinctions are being forced on the Cypriots by the speed of modern communications within small-scale communities where privacy and anonymity are difficult to achieve. But this change in society comes largely from the normal processes of development, as from a search for status in a newly independent nation. It is accompanied by a spread of urban, and Western, values and aspirations into the countryside, causing the beginnings of a breakdown in the close-knit family structure that has for so long dominated Cypriot life. It is amply illustrated by the fact that the Department of Social Welfare, covering the field of delinquency and destitution, child and family welfare, is now an essential part of government machinery. Moreover a number of homes for old people have been established in the main towns, fulfilling a need which would have been unimaginable not so many years ago.

These same developments must also be accompanied by a shift in the economic structure of the country, for an urban culture is barely compatible with the present arrangement whereby over half of the population are, directly or indirectly, dependent on agriculture for their living. There are few grounds for optimism that the mining industry will afford much economic growth: the reserves of copper are unlikely to last much beyond the 1970s; and asbestos, although present in substantial quantities, probably will not be fully exploited in the Troodos National Park. Tourism, too, even though more certain to expand well beyond the projected 400,000 arrivals in 1976, is maybe too fickle a source of earnings to be promoted at the expense of other sectors.

It must, then, fall to manufacturing industry to provide the basis for economic growth, at least over the next few decades. Craft industries have some scope for expansion before the traditional skills are completely lost; but they cannot form a large proportion of the total output. At the other end of the scale, it is difficult to visualise conditions under which heavy industry could become viable with such a small home market, although certain far-sighted entrepreneurs have been discussing the possibility of establishing a steel works on the south coast. The general conclusion, then, is that light manufacturing firms, initially concentrating on processing agricultural produce and on manufacturing clothing and footwear, will inevitably expand to provide a far greater number of jobs than at present. Looking further into the future, it may well be that Cyprus, given its geographical advantages, could become a communications centre of the eastern Mediterranean, or even farther afield; this, not only in terms of personal travel, but in the provision of computing and allied services as these become decentralised from more highly developed countries.

Although this is quite an encouraging picture, concern must be expressed about the future of the environment in Cyprus. Here, two conflicting forces are at work.

The first is manifested as the trend of industrialisation and urban development. It is, perhaps, fortunate that the towns and their commuter villages are not situated in the most attractive parts of the island—Kyrenia excepted, and Famagusta, whose one valuable natural asset, the beach, has in any case largely been spoiled beyond reclamation. For even though the form of development of the towns is unplanned and largely unco-ordinated, although the new architectural styles are, with a few minor exceptions, sadly unsympathetic to the old, and although the poorer people are being completely forced out of the towns by the high prices of land and building, the overall results—relatively orderly and far from being ugly—are greatly superior to those experienced in many (possibly most) other cities of the world today.

More alarming pressures are being felt in the villages, in the coastal areas and in the mountains. It may be unreasonable to expect all new houses to be constructed in traditional, but now expensive, styles. It would be equally unreasonable to expect that people should continue to live in the poor conditions of most existing village houses. But it is, at the same time, unfortunate that the more prosperous developers do not have a greater respect for indigenous architectural styles and materials; and that the old houses are not being maintained in such a way as to make them habitable in the second half of the twentieth century. As for the coast and the mountains, more and more is being lost daily to tourist 'development' on the one hand and to mining and military uses on the other. The deserted parts of the island are not the less useful on account of being economically unproductive.

On the positive side, however, sufficient damage has now been done to make public opinion aware of the dangers of overdevelopment and of the need for conservation. Examples of the new mood can be drawn from all quarters. Within the government, for a start, the Department of Forestry has an admirable record of awareness of the value of the environment; and the Departments of Town Planning and of Antiquities also contribute successfully in their own fields towards the preservation of the best of old Cyprus. Folk museums have been established in several places; and preservation of wild life, particularly of the birds of Cyprus, is being given a high priority by public and private bodies. National and local societies are springing up, pre-eminent among which is the Society of Cypriot Studies, recording the past and encouraging the development of a new national cultural awareness. A new type of Cypriot, too, is coming back to the island from foreign studies: despite higher financial rewards offered by employers elsewhere, they are staying at home to play their part in their country's development.

The overall picture, then, is neither one of unending violence nor one of a gloomy fall into economic and social patterns established decades earlier by Western nations. Change is inevitable, and must be welcomed as contributing towards an improvement in the standard and quality of living in the island. But the best of Cyprus will remain: no forces can entirely destroy its tranquil beauty; no one is going to demolish its historic buildings; and, above all, the warmth of its people is unchanging. The Greek word *Xenos* means 'Stranger' as well as 'Guest'; and it is this identity which, despite transitory turbulence, will continue to make Cyprus, above all, an island of peace.

CHRONOLOGY

5800–2500 BC	Neolithic Age
2500–2300 BC	Chalcolithic Age
2300–1050 BC	Bronze Age
(14th–12th centuries BC)	colonisation by Greeks
1000 BC	Start of Iron Age
800–550 BC	Assyrian and Egyptian periods
550–322 BC	Persian period
322–58 BC	Hellenistic period
58 BC–AD 395	Roman period
AD 45	missionary journey of Paul and Barnabas
325	Council of Nicaea
395–1191	Byzantine rule
478	autonomy of Church of Cyprus
647	death of Umm Haram
1100	foundation of Kykko Monastery
1191	Richard Coeur de Lion
1192–1489	Lusignan Dynasty
1231	martyrdom of thirteen Greek monks
1260	*Bulla Cypria*
1468	marriage of James II to Catherine of Cornaro
1489–1571	Venetian rule
1571–1878	Ottoman rule
1660	Archbishop recognised as Ethnarch
1821	Greek War of Independence; Archbishop Kyprianou hanged
1877	Russo-Turkish War

1878–1914	British Administration under the Suzerainty of the Sultans of Turkey
1913	birth of Michael Mouskos (Archbishop Makarios)
1914–25	British rule under the Crown
1925–60	British Crown Colony
1931	Government House, Nicosia, sacked
1947	Archbishop Leontios leads delegation to London
1950	Makarios III elected Archbishop
1954	first UN debate on Cyprus
1955	EOKA troubles start
1956	Radcliffe Commission on the Cyprus Constitution
1957–8	Makarios exiled to Seychelles
1959	London and Zurich agreements
1960	Republic of Cyprus
1963	Makarios suspends the constitution
1964	United Nations peacekeeping force (UNFICYP) arrives

PRINCIPAL HOLIDAYS AND FESTIVALS

Public Holidays

1 January	New Year's Day
6 January	Epiphany (Greek community only)
(40 days before Easter)	Green Monday (Greek)
19 January	Nameday of Archbishop Makarios (Greek)
25 March	Greek Independence Day (Greek)
(Movable)	Good Friday; Easter Saturday; Easter Monday (Greek)
23 April	Children's Bairam (Turkish)
19 May	Sports and Youth Bairam (Turkish)
30 August	Zafir Bairam (Turkish)
28 September	OCHI Day (Greek)
(Movable)	Birthday of the Prophet (Turkish)
(Movable)	Sheker Bairam, two days (Turkish)
(Movable)	Qurban Bairam, three days (Turkish)
25 December	Christmas Day (Greek)
26 December	Boxing Day (Greek)

Festivals

February	Famagusta Orange Festival
March, 50 days before Easter	Limassol Carnival
May	Flower Festival (mainly Paphos)
May, 50 days after Easter	Cataclysmos (mainly Larnaca)

August	Platres Festival
September	Curium Shakespeare Festival
September	Lapithos Lemon Festival
September	Nicosia International Trade Fair
September	Limassol Wine Festival

CLIMATIC TABLE

Nicosia, 1951–65

	Sunshine %	Rainfall (inches)	Max temp (°F)	Min temp (°F)
January	57	2·9	60	42
February	63	1·7	61	42
March	67	1·4	66	44
April	71	0·8	75	50
May	79	1·0	84	57
June	87	0·2	93	65
July	90	0·1	98	70
August	88	0·1	98	70
September	88	0·4	91	65
October	80	1·3	83	58
November	71	1·1	72	50
December	59	3·1	63	45

Mean monthly sea temperature (°F)

Jan	Feb	Mar	Apr	May	June	July	Aug	Sept	Oct	Nov	Dec
61	62	63	65	70	75	79	82	80	77	71	66

BIBLIOGRAPHY

All of the quotations in the text, whose authors are not listed below, are taken from *Excerpta Cypria: Materials for a History of Cyprus* by C. D. Cobham (Cambridge, 1908).

ABERCROMBIE, SIR P. *Preliminary Planning Report.* Nicosia, 1947
ALASTOS, DOROS. *Cyprus Guerilla.* 1960
——. *Cyprus in History.* 1955
ATTALIDES, M. A. *An Analysis of Urbanism in Cyprus with Special Reference to Nicosia.* Nicosia, 1970
BALFOUR, PATRICK. *The Orphaned Realm.* 1951
BANNERMAN, D. A. and W. M. *Birds of Cyprus.* Edinburgh, 1958
BARKER, DUDLEY. *Grivas, Portrait of a Terrorist.* 1959
BATTELLE MEMORIAL INSTITUTE. *Study of Industrial Development of Cyprus.* Geneva, 1963
BELLAMY, C. V. and JUKES-BROWN, A. J. *The Geology of Cyprus.* Plymouth, 1905
BOASE, T. S. R. *Kingdoms and Strongholds of the Crusaders.* 1971
CATLING, H. W. *Cyprus in the Neolithic and Bronze Age Periods.* Cambridge, 1968
CESNOLA, GENERAL A. P. D. *Cyprus: Its Ancient Cities, Tombs and Temples.* 1877
CHAPMAN, ESTHER F. *Cyprus Trees and Shrubs.* Nicosia, 1967
CHAPMAN, OLIVE MURRAY. *Across Cyprus.* 1945
CHRISTODOLOU, DEMETRIS. *The Evolution of the Rural Land Use Pattern in Cyprus.* 1959
CYPRUS TURKISH INFORMATION OFFICE. *The Cyprus Problem, A Brief Review.* Nicosia, 1970
DAWKINS, R. M., ed. *Leontios Makhaeras: Recital Concerning the Sweet Land of Cyprus, Entitled 'Chronicle'.* Oxford, 1932
DIKAIOS, P. *A Guide to the Cyprus Museum.* Nicosia, 1961
DIXON, W. HEPWORTH. *British Cyprus.* 1879
DURRELL, LAWRENCE. *Bitter Lemons.* 1957

BIBLIOGRAPHY

FOLEY, CHARLES. *Legacy of Strife.* 1964
GUNNIS, RUPERT. *Historic Cyprus.* 2nd ed, 1947
HACKETT, J. A. *A History of the Orthodox Church of Cyprus.* 1901
HADJICOSTA, ISMENE. *Cyprus and Its Life.* Nicosia, 1943
HAGGARD, RIDER H. *A Winter Pilgrimage: Being an Account of Travels through Palestine, Italy and the Island of Cyprus.* 1904
HALD, MARJORIE W. *A Study of the Cyprus Economy.* Nicosia, 1968
HARBOTTLE, MICHAEL. *The Impartial Soldier.* 1970
HILL, SIR GEORGE. *A History of Cyprus.* Cambridge, 1962
HOGARTH, D. G. *Devia Cypria.* 1889
HOLMBOE, J. *Studies on the Vegetation of Cyprus.* 1914
JEFFERY, GEORGE. *Historic Monuments of Cyprus.* Nicosia, 1918
JENNESS, DIAMOND. *The Economics of Cyprus: A Survey to 1914.* Montreal, 1962
KALLA-BISHOP, P. M. *Mediterranean Island Railways.* Newton Abbot, 1970
KARAGEORGHIS, V. *Cyprus: Archaeologia Mundi.* Geneva, 1968
——. *Treasures in the Cyprus Museum.* Nicosia, 1962
KESHISHIAN, KEVORK K. *Romantic Cyprus.* 1970
KOUMOULIDES, JOHN T. A. *Cyprus and the War of Greek Independence 1821–1829.* Athens, 1971
LUKE, SIR HARRY. *Cyprus.* 1957
——. *Cyprus under the Turks.* 1921
MARITI, GIO. *Travels in the Island of Cyprus.* Reprinted 1971
MATTHEWS, ANN. *Lilies of the Field.* Limassol, 1968
MEYER, A. J. with VASSILIOU, S. *The Economy of Cyprus.* Cambridge, Mass., 1962
NEWMAN, PHILIP. *A Short History of Cyprus.* 1940
ORR, C. W. J. *Cyprus under British Rule.* 1918
PANAYIDES, S. *An Econometric Study of the Cyprus Economy.* Iowa, 1967
PAPAGEORGHIOU, ATHANASIUS. *Icons of Cyprus.* 1969
PARKER, ROBIN. *Aphrodite's Realm.* Nicosia, 1968
POLUNIN, OLEG and HUXLEY, ANTHONY. *Flowers of the Mediterranean.* 1965
SITAS, A. *Kopiaste.* Limassol, 1968
SPYRIDAKIS, C. *A Brief History of Cyprus.* Nicosia, 1948
STEPHENS, ROBERT. *Cyprus, A Place of Arms.* 1966
STYLIANOU, ANDREAS. *The Painted Churches of Cyprus.* 1964
STYLIANOU, ANDREAS and JUDITH A. *Byzantine Cyprus.* Nicosia, 1948
TALBOT RICE, D. *The Icons of Cyprus.* 1937
THURSTON, HAZEL. *The Travellers' Guide to Cyprus.* 1967

Toy, Barbara. *Rendezvous in Cyprus.* 1970
United Nations. *Cyprus—Suggestions for a Development Programme.*
  New York, 1961
Vanezis, Dr P. N. *Makarios: Faith and Power.* 1971

Periodicals and Occasional Cyprus Government Publications

Archaeologia Viva. March 1969
Cyprus Mail
Cyprus Today
Cyprus, The Problem in Perspective. PIO, Nicosia, 1969
The Mineral Resources and Mining Industry of Cyprus. 1963
Second Five-Year Plan, 1967–71
Censuses of 1946 and 1960
Demographic Reports
Economic Reports
Statistical Abstracts

ACKNOWLEDGEMENTS

During the two short years that we lived in Cyprus, we pestered all of our Cypriot friends with questions until they must have become heartily sick of our interrogations. Nevertheless, they endured with patience and goodwill; and provided us with a good basis for our understanding of how and why Cyprus is what it is today. Thanks, then, to all of our friends, Greek and Turkish Cypriots, who made this book possible.

The greatest thanks must go to the Cyprus Government for employing one of us and thus giving us both the opportunity to live in such a beautiful and interesting island—but it must be made clear that the views expressed in the preceding pages do not necessarily reflect official positions.

Acknowledgements are due to *Cyprus Today* for permission to reproduce the poem by Costas Montis at the beginning of Chapter 2.

We should, too, like to express our deep gratitude to four people without whose specific help this book would never have been written. The first is Dr J. B. Harley, the editor of this Islands Series, for his patience and co-operation during all stages of its preparation. Next come Francis and Helen Suttill, colleagues of ours in Cyprus, with whom we were able to share much of our enthusiasm for the delights of the island. Finally, and perhaps most importantly, Jack Waterton Lee, who patiently and even willingly lent us all his facilities for the writing of the book.

INDEX

Page numbers in italic indicate illustrations

INDEX

206